MW01504651

"God's Healing Secrets is a truth. God intends for h made every provision Krstevski presents God's intention and God's instructions regarding our health in a straightforward and faith-building way. Sometimes it takes someone reminding us what is already in our 'Heavenly Health Plan' and Dr. Krstevski has accomplished this for us with clarity. Dr. Krstevski's personal insights and experiences will be an encouragement to you to take hold of God's Health Plan. I feel healthier just for having read the truths presented in this book. I recommend this book not only to those who need to receive healing, but to everyone who would like to live their 120 years with health and vibrancy."

—REV. JONATHAN KRENZ
Senior Pastor, Victory Church on the Rock, Edmonton, AB

"Dr. Slobodan Krstevski's book presents a totally integrated viewpoint on healing."

—JIM FISHER
Businessman, Burlington, ON

"In this easy-to-understand book, Dr. Slobodan Krstevski teaches physical, mental, and spiritual principles for divine health. I encourage everyone to read this book and apply its biblically-based teachings in order to see the great benefits of healthy living, both in body and spirit."

—GORDON KLASSEN
Vice-President of Corporate Affairs, The Miracle Channel

"In his book, *God's Healing Secrets*, Dr. Slobodan Krstevski gives balanced answers to issues of divine and natural healing. By examining the healing ministry in the Old Testament, of Jesus, and of the Early Church, Dr. Krstevski provides a biblical basis for his belief in divine healing. Everyone who reads and applies the principles laid out in this book could greatly benefit both in his spiritual and physical well-being."

—REV. JACK OZARD
Former Regional Director East, WOD, PAOC

"I have personally applied some of the biblical truths on healing spoken about in Dr. Slobodan Krstevski's book and I was healed. Jesus healed me from various sicknesses. I believe that God is good and that He wants people to be healthy, especially those who want to claim it by faith in Him. During my family medical practice as a doctor working with patients, I have applied the biblical principles of healing. I have seen that God healed them and extended lives to many through my prayers. I recommend this book, which especially speaks of God's principles of healing."

—DR. IRENA VITANOVSKA, MD
Ihtus Remedium Christian Clinic, Skopje, Macedonia

"Slobodan, I found your book, *God's Healing Secrets*, to be a wonderful guide for everybody who needs health, both in the physical and spiritual sense."

—DR. BENITO MUÑOZ, MD
Star-Med Clinic and Spa, Tijuana, Mexico

"*God's Healing Secrets* tells of the success one can have by combining everything we have been doing for so many years and that is mind, body, and soul restoration and rejuvenation. Bravo, Slobodan, for giving the world the meaning of WHOLISTIC!"

—THOMAS PETERSEN, RN
Natural Therapies and Spa, Tijuana, Mexico

GOD'S
HEALING
SECRETS

Dr. Slobodan Krstevski, Ph.D.

GOD'S HEALING SECRETS

Unless otherwise indicated, all Scripture quotations are taken from the Holy Bible, King James Version, which is in the public domain. Scripture quotations marked NASB are taken from the New American Standard Bible®, Copyright © 1960, 1962, 1963, 1968, 1971, 1972, 1973, 1975, 1977, 1995 by The Lockman Foundation. Used by permission. Scripture quotations marked AMP are taken from the Amplified Bible, Copyright © 1954, 1958, 1962, 1964, 1965, 1987 by The Lockman Foundation. Used by permission. Scripture quotations marked NKJV are taken from the New King James Version®. Copyright © 1982 by Thomas Nelson, Inc. Used by permission. All rights reserved. Scripture quotations marked NLT are taken from the Holy Bible, New Living Translation, copyright 1996, 2004. Used by permission of Tyndale House Publishers, Inc., Wheaton, Illinois 60189. All rights reserved. Scripture quotations marked NIV are taken from the Holy Bible, New International Version®. Copyright © 1973, 1978, 1984 by Biblica, Inc.™ Used by permission of Zondervan. All rights reserved worldwide.

ISBN-13: 978-1-77069-077-6

Printed in Canada.

Word Alive Press
131 Cordite Road, Winnipeg, MB R3W 1S1
www.wordalivepress.ca

WORD ALIVE PRESS
Just Write!

The purpose of this book is to reveal principles from the Word of God and teach how you can apply those principles to receive healing. This book is not intended to provide medical advice or to take the place of medical advice and treatment from your personal physician. Readers are advised to consult their own doctors or other qualified health professionals regarding the treatment of their health problems. Neither the publisher nor the author takes any responsibility for any possible consequences from any treatment, action or application of medicine, supplement, herb or preparation to any person reading or following the information in this book. If readers are taking prescription medications, they should consult with their physicians and not take themselves off the medication to start supplementation without the proper supervision of a qualified physician.

God's Word says:

"That thy way may be known upon earth, thy saving health among all nations" (Psalm 67:2).

"For I will restore health unto thee, and I will heal thee of thy wounds, saith the LORD" (Jeremiah 30:17a).

"Bless the LORD, O my soul: and all that is within me, bless his holy name. Bless the LORD, O my soul, and forget not all his benefits: Who forgiveth all thine iniquities; who healeth all thy diseases; Who redeemeth thy life from destruction; who crowneth thee with lovingkindness and tender mercies; Who satisfieth thy mouth with good things; so that thy youth is renewed like the eagle's" (Psalm 103:1–5).

In gratitude to God, I dedicate this book to every person who wants to be healthy in his or her body, soul, and spirit and who is willing to embrace both God's element of the supernatural ways of healing and our natural responsibilities in order to be healed.

"For I am the LORD that healeth thee"
(Exodus 15:26c).

"With his stripes we are healed" (Isaiah 53:5).

"The fruit thereof shall be for meat, and the leaf thereof for medicine" (Ezekiel 47:12c).

"Our food should be our medicine.
Our medicine should be our food"
—Hippocrates, the Father of Modern Medicine
(460–377 BC).

TABLE OF CONTENTS

TABLE OF CONTENTS

PREFACE

In our ministry, both here in North America and in Europe, we meet a lot of families and individuals who are in need of healing. Actually, most of the responses to our daily television broadcasts are from our partners who have prayer requests for physical healing, either for themselves or someone they love.

At Shining Light Ministries, we consider our ministry to be one that serves families. We wrote a book entitled *Bless Your Children to Succeed* because we wanted to bless parents with tools they can use to raise their children with godliness and success, so that they may become wise and mighty in spirit.

My wife Ljiljana and I have six children, and the principles we've employed in raising them have brought great results in how they're maturing. We believe those same principles can be used by other parents so they, too, can bless their children to succeed. The book even won an award from The Word Guild as the best book by a Christian author in Canada on the subject of parenting.

We wrote another book, entitled *From the Curse of Debt to Financial Freedom: Seven Principles of Prosperity*. We realized that a lot of families are struggling with their finances and that it is one of the major causes of divorce today. It seems every month families are running out of money before they run out of days. So in that book, we laid out principles for not only getting out of debt, but also for becoming prosperous. We know that God wants us to prosper in every area of our lives, including our finances.

Then we noticed that, aside from parenting issues and financial difficulties, a lot of families are dealing with problems resulting from their marital conflicts. It seems a lot of couples don't know how to relate to each other in a loving, considerate, and nurturing way, especially after being married for many years. As a result, many of them are getting divorced. After financial problems, adultery is the second greatest cause for divorce. So we wrote a book called *His and Her Cup of Love: Seven Steps to a Great Marriage* because we wanted to minister to married couples. We wanted to teach couples how to nurture and enjoy their marriages. That book also won an award from The Word Guild in Canada.

After writing those three books, it seemed we had provided resources for every aspect of family life: parenting, finances, and marriage. But then we noticed one thing many of our partners still struggled with—their health. A lot of people, both young and old, expect to be sick and unhealthy as they get older. Biblically speaking, there is no need for that. So we felt we needed to write this book, *God's Healing Secrets*. Our daughter Elisabeth, who at the time was only nine years old, gave us the idea for the title of this book.

I believe there are *supernatural* ways of healing through the divine power of our awesome God. But I also believe there is a *natural* element to healing, meaning there are natural things that we need to do if we are to walk in divine health.

I believe God intended for us to live 120 years and live those years with health and vibrancy (Genesis 6:3). The reason most people don't reach this age today is that they neglect their own spiritual, emotional, and physical well-being. This book's purpose is to provide you with knowledge and insight to help you understand how you can receive healing, both from a supernatural perspective and from a natural perspective. If you are to become healthy and well, you need to employ both of these spiritual and natural elements of divine health.

I would not have been able to write this book had I not experienced these issues personally. I want to thank my wife, Ljiljana, who has been very supportive of me throughout our marriage, ever since we married on July 7, 1984, and especially through this journey toward improving our health. Together we have been able to apply the principles discussed in this book, and now both of us (and all of our children) are walking in divine health!

Above all, I want to thank God for the insight that He has given me and for the information that I have learned from both the Scriptures and other godly people. I praise and thank my Lord and Saviour Jesus Christ, my Healer, for teaching me how to walk in divine health.

My desire and prayer is for you to be walking in divine health as well. God wants you to be healed, and He wants you to be healed in your body, soul, and spirit. When God heals, He heals completely. He never leaves anything out. In the Gospels, we read about the works of Jesus and we notice that everybody who ever came to Jesus for healing received what they came for. Jesus never refused to heal anybody.

So I want to encourage you not to accept any sickness as a "final say" in your life but to declare that you are free from sickness and blessed with divine health in your body, soul, and spirit in the name of Jesus Christ, the Son of the living God. Seek the Lord's guidance as to what you might need to do both from the natural and spiritual perspectives. Let me finish by quoting 3 John 1:2: *"Beloved, I wish above all things that thou mayest prosper and be in health, even as thy soul prospereth."*

INTRODUCTION

There are certain things in life that are free of charge, and those are the best things in life. For example, our life did not cost us anything. It was given to us as a gift from God. We didn't have to pay for it. Our spouse and our children have been given to us as gifts from God. Forgiveness of our sins is a true gift from God. And most of us have received health as a gift from God.

Other things in life cost money, such as our house, car, food, clothing, and vacations. All of those things are less important than the free things that God has given us. Yet it's interesting that we sometimes lose our priorities and start focusing on things that cost money (the less important things) rather than the things that don't cost money (the more important things) like our marriages, our children, and even our life and health. It shouldn't be like that. We should really set proper priorities for ourselves.

There are many people who are sick, including Christians. In Chapter One, I will answer the question of why Christians get sick. Sometimes it's because of our disobedience to the clear teachings in the Word of God. If God teaches us to live a certain way but we choose to live in disobedience, we are going to reap the consequences of our actions, one of which could be sickness. Other times we could be sick because we don't have the knowledge that's required to be healthy. Or perhaps we are sick because we've made some wrongful confessions over our lives, such as speaking sickness and death over ourselves.

Then in Chapter Two, I will talk about the spirit and God's supernatural healing. There are Old Testament teachings about healing, and there are New Testament teachings about healing that Jesus gave when He was on the earth. Also, as we study the book of Acts, we'll see that the apostles had a healing ministry as well. And when Jesus went to heaven, He commissioned all of us, as believers, to be engaged in a healing ministry, too.

After that, we will move on to Chapter Three, where I will talk about the soul and how to receive God's supernatural healing. It's interesting how forgiveness usually precedes healing. There are some emotional issues that God wants us to deal with before we experience divine health. About ninety percent of all sicknesses are caused by emotional imbalance. We'll also talk about how healing comes through the Word of God, the practice of laying hands on people, and the importance of prayer and faith in receiving God's supernatural healing.

Once we look at the supernatural element of healing and how to receive that supernatural healing, we'll discuss some natural ways of healing in Chapter Four. These are steps that we have to apply in our lives in order to continue walking in divine health after we've been healed, or sometimes even to receive our healing. God wants to prosper us, but He blesses the effort of our hands (Deuteronomy 28:8). No effort, no blessing! There are things that we're required to do, things that God will not do for us. God gave the Israelites the Promised Land, but they had to go and fight for it. In other words, there are some things that we have to do for our healing to come, and nobody else will do those things for us, not even God Himself.

When people are sick, they often turn to medicine, but the purpose of medicine is not to heal or cure a sickness. I do not speak against medicine, but medicine does have its limits. The best results we can hope from medicine are for it to control a sickness and hopefully stop it from spreading. But often the various combinations of medicine can harm your health more than help it. The same can be said about various types of surgeries. For that reason, I will talk about important things we need to do for natural healing, such as reducing stress, drinking enough filtered water, eating living food and not dead food, getting enough rest, exercising regularly, detoxifying our bodies, and taking supplements.

Also in Chapter Four, I will talk about proper methods for losing weight. My wife Ljiljana and I struggled with our weights for almost a decade. We've learned over the years that diets and fasting don't work. When we discovered what *did* work, we applied it in our lives and saw rapid results. So in that chapter, we share how you, too, can lose weight in a healthy way (if you feel you need to) and keep that weight off.

Then in Chapter Five, I'll talk about the importance of positive confessions. Everything starts with the words that come out of your mouth. What you say about your abilities or disabilities will determine what you can do. What you say about sickness or health will determine your physical well-being. It all starts with the words you speak. I'll talk more specifically about the power of the tongue, how your words determine your destiny, and the importance of speaking life into your situations. I also provide you with a very powerful and encouraging personal confession that you can make to declare the start of your journey from sickness to health.

At the end of the book, you'll find wonderful scriptures on healing. I encourage you to learn some of those verses by heart. Write them down on pieces of paper that you can hang on your fridge, by your desk at the office, near your bed, or on the dashboard in your car. That way, you can read those verses regarding your health and well-being and make confessions based on them on a regular basis. Also, you'll find my personal healing story. I was healed from prostate cancer by declaring those things that are not as though they are and by applying natural ways to accomplish positive results. I hope that my story will inspire your faith in the Word of God, so that you may start believing, speaking, and doing what it takes to see supernatural healing come to pass in *your own* life.

It says in Jeremiah 1:12, *"Then the LORD said to me, 'You have seen well, for I am watching over My word to perform it'"* (NASB). God watches over His Word to perform it, meaning He will do exactly what He says He will do. So when you and I speak the Word of God back to Him, God is going to make sure He performs everything we speak because we're speaking His Word.

I encourage you to prayerfully read this book and apply the principles I discuss in your own life. My wife and I have applied these strategies, and as a result we've successfully improved our health. We are walking in divine health. You can do the same! The journey from sickness to health doesn't have to be difficult. Just follow the instructions in this book and obey the wisdom found in the Word of God, and in time you'll get there!

CHAPTER ONE
Why Do Christians Get Sick?

*"Know ye not that ye are the temple of God, and that
the Spirit of God dwelleth in you? If any man defile
the temple of God, him shall God destroy; for the
temple of God is holy, which temple ye are"*
(1 Corinthians 3:16–17).

According to the above verses, our bodies are the temple of the Holy Spirit. It's so important to understand that, as Christians, our bodies are not our own; they belong to God. And if we abuse or defile our bodies, our bodies are going to be destroyed.

It seems that very few people associate their actions with the well-being of their bodies. I believe that about ninety percent of all sicknesses Christians experience have come about because we've violated natural laws that God has put in place. This is especially true when we don't take care of the temple of God. That's one of the reasons why Christians are sick.

I believe that sickness and disease are not necessary and can and should be avoided. God has not created our bodies for sickness but for health. I think as Christians we should ask ourselves, "Is it possible that we don't have to experience heart attacks, strokes, cancer, or diabetes? Can we really stop having headaches, allergies, arthritic pains, and other sicknesses?" Those are very legitimate questions to ask.

"For whatever a man sows, that and that only is what he will reap."
—Galatians 6:7c, AMP

It says in 2 Timothy 3:16, *"All scripture is given by inspiration of God, and is profitable for doctrine, for reproof, for correction, for instruction in righteousness."* So if we want to learn how to live healthy, we need to know the Word of God. God's Word provides us with wisdom to properly manage every area of our lives, including our health. It says in Psalm 139:14, *"I will praise thee; for I am fearfully and wonderfully made: marvellous are thy works; and that my soul knoweth right well."* God has created our bodies in such a unique, complex way.

Did you know that our bodies consist of about one hundred trillion cells? Those cells require constant nourishment, constant rebuilding, and constant cleansing from contaminants. They are usually renewed every week at a rate of three hundred million cells per minute. Much of our bodies are rebuilt every year. Even our bones are rebuilt and renewed within several years. That's why it's so important to give our bodies the proper nourishment and cleansing they need. There's no reason we should have sicknesses in our bodies.

Let's talk about blood, for example. A human body has about five litres of blood, and that blood is constantly travelling within our bodies, making about three to five thousand round trips every day. Did you know that the heart pumps about twenty billion blood cells throughout the body? These blood cells carry nourishment to every cell in the body. At the same time, they remove toxins and waste. That's why it's so important that we keep our hearts strong, and that's where exercise comes in, which I will discuss in more detail later.

There is so much to learn about how to keep the temple of God healthy. In this book, I'll discuss various ways of receiving healing, both supernaturally and naturally. But for now, let's explore the Word of God and learn some of the reasons why Christians are sick.

I'm sure we've all heard or asked the question, "Why does God allow bad things to happen to good people?" Have you ever wondered about that? The answer is simple. You reap what you sow. In the Amplified Bible, Galatians 6:7c says, *"For whatever a man sows, that and that only is what he will reap"* (AMP). I believe most, albeit not all, Christians who are currently dealing with illnesses became sick for one of three reasons: disobedience to God, lack of knowledge, or wrongful confessions.

Disobedience to God

"But it shall come to pass, if thou wilt not hearken unto the voice of the LORD thy God, to observe to do all his commandments and his statutes which I command thee this day; that all these curses shall come upon thee, and overtake thee" (Deuteronomy 28:15).

In Deuteronomy 28:1–14, we read about all the blessings that God will bestow upon those who obey Him. Then in verses 15–58, we read about all the curses that will come upon those who disobey Him. It's interesting to notice that sickness is not in the column of blessings from God. All sicknesses and diseases are considered curses, and the reason some people experience curses in their lives is that they've been disobedient to God or violated some of His Word.

God cannot keep us healthy if we disobey His Word. When we walk in disobedience to God's commandments, we are connecting ourselves to Satan and allowing ourselves to be an open target for Satan to attack. One of his attacks could be in the form of sickness. When we are living in sin, we are not allowing God to protect us from sickness. For example, if we engage in immoral acts such as promiscuity, using drugs, or drinking alcohol, God cannot protect us from the consequences of those actions. Ultimately, we will reap the destruction of those sins.

I believe that if we confess our sins and live a godly lifestyle, eighty percent of sicknesses will never come to us and the other twenty percent of sicknesses that could come to us will be healed when we ask God to heal us.

On the other hand, if we walk in obedience to God's commandments, we are connecting ourselves to God. As a result, we will be invoking God's blessing and protection in our lives. Obedience brings blessings, while disobedience brings curses.

I believe almost eighty percent of sicknesses that people experience are a direct result of sin. Think of all the sexually transmitted diseases, for example. Many people catch viruses and infections by committing fornication and adultery. Some people suffer with lung cancer as a result of smoking cigarettes. Other people experience liver and kidney damage because of excessive alcohol consumption. There are people who have neurological damage as a result of drug use.

This may be a surprise to some, but some sicknesses are caused by feelings of bitterness and resentment. When resentment comes into your heart, that resentment puts stress on your body, which in turn weakens your immune system. So when a virus tries to attack your body, your immune system isn't strong enough to fight

Acidity in your body is the major culprit of inflammation, and inflammation is a major source of sickness.

that virus off. That's why many bitter and resentful people become easily sick. When you stay bitter and resentful toward someone, you're allowing that person to control your life, and even your health. If you forgive that person, you will be set free from his or her control.

Some of the health problems you experience could be stress-related. Perhaps you are taking on too many responsibilities at work. Or maybe you're not prioritizing your time or money properly. Stress can cause acidity to build up in your body. Acidity in your body is the major culprit of inflammation, and inflammation is a major source of sickness. So there are all kinds of illnesses that are derived from sin.

But I believe that if we confess our sins and live a godly lifestyle, eighty percent of sicknesses will never come to us and the other twenty percent of sicknesses that *could* come to us will be healed when we ask God to heal us. When we are walking in obedience to God, we will experience God's healing power in our lives.

Some sicknesses are caused by feelings of bitterness and resentment.

We read in 1 Corinthians 11:28–32, *"But let a man examine himself, and so let him eat of that bread, and drink of that cup. For he that eateth and drinketh unworthily, eateth and drinketh damnation to himself, not discerning the Lord's body. For this cause many are weak and sickly among you, and many sleep. For if we would judge ourselves, we should not be judged. But when we are judged, we are chastened of the Lord, that we should not be condemned with the world."* We ought to judge ourselves, meaning we have to examine our lifestyles to see if they are in line with God's Word. That's so important to do if we are to keep our bodies strong and healthy, as opposed to weak and sickly.

But let me clarify that I'm not saying all sicknesses are a result of sin. We read in John 9:1–3, *"And as Jesus passed by, he saw a man which was blind from his birth. And his disciples asked him, saying, Master, who did sin, this man, or his parents, that he was born blind? Jesus answered, Neither hath this man sinned, nor his parents: but that the works of God should be made manifest in him."*

In this case, this man's sickness wasn't because of sin; it could have had genetic roots. This was a sickness through which God wanted to be glorified. Not all sicknesses are a result of sin. There could be other reasons, which I will discuss shortly. The cause isn't always sin, but sin—and especially a sinful lifestyle—can occasionally be the root of some sicknesses.

There are many sick Christians who regularly receive prayer for healing but never seem to receive their healing. Why is that? It could be because they live in disobedience. They need to restore their spiritual health first before God can restore their physical health (3 John 1:2). If that is the case in your situation, don't be discouraged.

We read in 1 John 1:9, *"If we confess our sins, he is faithful and just to forgive us our sins, and to cleanse us from all unrighteousness."* If you know you've become ill because of a past sin, also know that you can come before God, confess your sins to Him, and He will be faithful and just to forgive you of your sins and cleanse you from all unrighteousness. Once the sin is removed, most of the time the sickness will be removed also.

Lack of Knowledge

"My people are destroyed for lack of knowledge" (Hosea 4:6a).

Knowledge is so important. Without knowledge, people fall into disastrous situations in their lives, whether it is spiritually, relationally, financially, or even regarding their health. Today, we live in an age of information. Those who have knowledge will move forward in life and be successful, while those who lack knowledge will lack in life. Knowledge is very important for success. Knowledge is power. When people increase in knowledge, they increase in power as well.

That is exactly what we read in Proverbs 24:5: *"A wise man is strong; yea, a man of knowledge increaseth strength."* A man who has wisdom is a man who has skills. He is also shrewd and prudent. He knows how to act in accordance with the wisdom of God. That person is strong. A man who has knowledge is a man who learns and

Eating dead food only leads to death... Eating living food brings life.

educates himself to become better. That man increases in strength, ability, and might. So having both knowledge and wisdom can only bring benefits, but not having knowledge will cause us to perish (Hosea 4:6a).

There are many people who lack knowledge about what constitutes a healthy lifestyle. For example, some people don't know much about

proper eating habits, so they eat junk food, such as fried foods and processed foods.

In 1 Timothy 4:4, we read a passage about food: *"For everything God
has created is good, and nothing is to be thrown away or refused if it is received
with thanksgiving"* (AMP). Food that God has created is good. It's much
better than the food man processes, which has lost most of its nutrients
because man has overcooked it or deep-fried it. That food is dead because all the enzymes (nutrients) are dead.

Eating dead food only leads to death. But when we eat living food,
such as fresh fruits and vegetables in their raw state, we're eating the
good food that God has created. Eating living food brings life. Many
people don't know this, and as a result they eat unhealthy food, which
in turn leads to health problems. (I discuss more about eating living food
in Chapter Four.)

Some people may know about the importance of a healthy diet, but
they only know it in theory—not in practice. If we don't practice what
we say we know, we really don't know it. For example, if we say we
know what it takes to be healthy but we don't eat proper foods, then we
really don't know how to be healthy. Our actions speak a lot louder
than our words. We show that we have knowledge about something by
practicing it in our daily lives. It says in James 4:17, *"Therefore to him that
knoweth to do good, and doeth it not, to him it is sin."* If we know what is
right to do but choose not to do it, that is considered sin. That disobedience will only lead us to death and destruction.

Other things that many people don't have much knowledge about
are the negative effects of white flour, sugar, and salt. Let's talk about
white flour first. White flour is made by removing the germ of the
wheat, which contains most of the nutrients of the wheat. After the
germ is removed, the bran gets taken out, because the bran leaves behind brown specs in the flour. (It's interesting to note that both the
wheat germ and wheat bran get sold later on in health food stores.)

Once the germ and the bran are removed, whatever is left over gets
bleached using chemical bleaching agents like Clorox. That's what

makes the flour look nice and white. After the flour is bleached, coal- and tar-derived vitamins get added to it. Then the flour gets packaged and sold to consumers. At this point, there is no nutritional value in the white flour we buy in the stores.

Let's talk about sugar now. Sugar is naturally found in sugar beets and sugar canes. But we do not get sugar in its natural state. Natural sugar gets refined in a fourteen-step process. During that process, the refiners remove the B-complex, enzymes, proteins, minerals, and vitamins found in natural sugar. When the processing is finished, we get a product that is devitalized of chemical substance and contains no vitamins, minerals, or God-given nutrients. It is just pure carbohydrates.

Sugar is capable of doing great damage to our bodies. Even though God created sugar, when we get it after the devitalizing process, it can really be dangerous to our bodies. Some of the symptoms of hypergly- cemia, which is a result of too much sugar, are headaches, irritability, depression, fatigue, lack of concentration, and becoming easily upset with loved ones, often for no valid reason. Sugar leaches vitamin B out of our bodies, depletes calcium, and really works on destroying our nervous system. Stevia extract is a much better choice in place of sugar.

If we continue adding white flour, sugar, salt, and other harmful compounds to our diets, eventually we will destroy our bodies.

Another compound that is harmful to our health is salt. Salt in the form of sodium chloride is one of the greatest killers of humanity. Both earth and sea salts are inorganic forms of sodium that our bodies cannot utilize. In other words, those salts enter our bodies but cannot be eliminated through our urine or sweat glands. So that salt gets stored in the tissue of the body as sodium chloride. Sodium chloride draws water from the bloodstream and that water helps to dilute that salt concentration in order to neutralize the poison of the salt in the body.

WHY DO CHRISTIANS GET SICK?

There are various physical problems that are caused by high salt intake, such as hardening of the arteries, arthritic pain, ulcers, vision problems, high blood pressure, tumours, cancers, and other degenerative diseases. When you put salt in your food, you actually take the flavour and nutrients out of your food. You don't taste the food anymore; you taste the salt. All the salt our bodies need can be taken from organic, naturally grown fruits and vegetables. We do not need to add salt to our food.

It says in Galatians 6:7, *"For whatever a man sows, that and that only is what he will reap"* (AMP). So if we continue adding white flour, sugar, salt, and other harmful compounds to our diets, eventually we will destroy our bodies. However, many people don't know how harmful these foods can be. As a result, they don't control their intake of them. When they consume too much, they experience the negative consequences linked with those actions. If you're sick and wondering how you got sick, examine your eating habits. You may have gotten sick because you lacked knowledge regarding the types of food that are destructive to your body.

Wrongful Confessions

"Death and life are in the power of the tongue: and they that love it shall eat the fruit thereof" (Proverbs 18:21).

People are not sick because God inflicted sicknesses upon them. Sicknesses don't come from God. Since they don't come from God, they must have another source. If God is the source of all goodness, Satan must be the source of all evil. Satan is a demonic power, a spirit that tries to take away everything God wants to give you. Satan is not there to bless you, but to destroy you.

In Deuteronomy 28:1–14,

Sickness is a destructive element that Satan uses to destroy your body. The longer you keep confessing it's yours, the longer you're going to have to deal with it.

9

we read about the blessings of God. As I said, there is no mention of sickness there. Sickness is not in the column of blessings. Sickness is in the column of curses. So if sickness is a curse, why are so many Christians sick? Aside from disobedience to God and lack of knowledge, another reason could be wrongful confessions.

According to the above verse, life and death are found in the power of the tongue. I often hear people say, "*My* arthritis is bothering me again," or "I need prayer for *my* cancer." Why do you own that sickness? Did you buy it? Is it a treasured possession? Do you need to declare that it belongs to you? God does not want you to be sick. He wants you to be healed and well. In 3 John 1:2 we read, "*Beloved, I wish above all things that thou mayest prosper and be in health, even as thy soul prospereth.*" Whenever Jesus encountered sick people, He healed them all (Matthew 11:5).

If there's a sickness in your body, it's important to understand that God didn't give you that sickness. That sickness is a destructive element that Satan uses to destroy your body. The longer you keep confessing it's yours, the longer you're going to have to deal with it. Your body is the temple of the Holy Spirit and God wants it well. So you should never claim ownership over a sickness. Instead, you need to declare to the spirit of sickness that it has no authority to be in your body.

Other times, I hear Christians make wrongful confessions about how long they're going to live. Some Christians have quoted Psalm 90:10: "*The days of our lives are seventy years; and if by reason of strength they are eighty years, yet their boast is only labor and sorrow; for it is soon cut off, and we fly away*" (NKJV). According to the context of this verse, the seventy- or eighty-year lifespan mentioned here is actually the lifespan of a sinful person, a person who walks in disobedience to God.

In Genesis 6:3 we read, "*And the LORD said, My spirit shall not always strive with man, for that he also is flesh: yet his days shall be an hundred and twenty years.*" God has given man a lifespan of 120 years. That was the lifespan that God intended for us to live after the flood.

Actually, modern medical science confirms that a human being should live about that length of time. The founder and president of the American Academy of Anti-Aging Medicine, Dr. Ronald Klatz, said, "Over half of the baby boomers here in America are going to see their hundredth birthday and beyond in excellent health. We're looking at life spans for the baby boomers and the generation after the baby boomers of 120 to 150 years of age."[1] If we're walking in obedience to God and taking proper care of our physical bodies, we have every right to expect to be healthy and live vibrantly until the age of 120.

If we're walking in obedience to God and taking proper care of our physical bodies, we have every right to expect to be healthy and live vibrantly until the age of 120.

In Deuteronomy 34:7 we read, *"Moses was 120 years old when he died, yet his eyesight was clear, and he was as strong as ever"* (NLT). Moses died as a strong, healthy 120-year-old man. He probably could have still continued living, but God decided that it was time for him to go, so he went.

In Joshua 14:10–11 Caleb said, *"And now, behold, the LORD has kept me alive, as He said, these forty-five years, ever since the LORD spoke this word to Moses while Israel wandered in the wilderness; and now, here I am this day, eighty-five years old. As yet I am as strong this day as on the day that Moses sent me; just as my strength was then, so now is my strength for war, both for going out and for coming in"* (NKJV). Caleb was eighty-five years old when he entered into the Promised Land, but he declared that he was still strong and healthy even in his old age.

God doesn't want us to lose our health as we age, and He certainly doesn't want us to die young. We can see in the Scriptures that God desires for us to live long, healthy, vibrant lives. It's so important that we make the right confessions about the health of our bodies and how long we're going to live.

If you confess that you're going to be sick or you're going to die young, you'll likely end up getting exactly what you have spoken. We read earlier in Proverbs 18:21, *"Death and life are in the power of the tongue: and they that love it shall eat the fruit thereof."* Whether or not you experience death or life is controlled by the words you speak. What a powerful truth.

If you're sick, I encourage you to take a few moments to examine yourself. I've just discussed three possible reasons for your sickness. Perhaps you can relate your situation to one or more of the reasons I mentioned. Maybe you've strayed away from God and started engaging in some things you know you shouldn't be engaged in. Or perhaps you've fed your body the wrong foods without knowing the harmful effects those foods can have. Or maybe you've made some negative confessions over your health and now your confessions have come to pass in the form of a sickness.

Whatever the reason may be, now is the time to be honest with yourself and make a new beginning in your life. This is the beginning of your journey from sickness to health. If you've been disobedient to God, go to God in prayer and confess your sins. If you've made some mistakes because of a lack of knowledge, educate yourself. And if you've made some wrongful confessions, start making the right ones. This book has been designed to walk you through repairing the consequences of each of those three actions so that you may receive your healing.

Now that you know the main reasons for most sicknesses, let's move on to discuss God's supernatural healing power. We serve a God who is mighty and powerful, a God who is able to heal any and every sickness. Nothing is impossible for Him (Luke 1:37). He is the One who created our bodies, so He is more than able and willing to heal our bodies.

In Chapter Two, we will discuss the spiritual aspect of healing. We'll explore the Scriptures to learn more about God's supernatural healing in the Old Testament, the New Testament, and today. If we are to experience God's healing in our lives, we need to learn how His healing has been manifested throughout history. So let us proceed to the next chapter together and discover more about the power of our awesome *Jehovah Rophe*—the Lord our Healer (Exodus 15:26b)!

CHAPTER TWO
Spirit: God's Supernatural Healing

"For I will restore health unto thee, and I will heal
thee of thy wounds, saith the LORD"
(Jeremiah 30:17a).

God is the Healer. It was never the intention of our loving God for people to be sick. It's important to recognize that the source of healing is the Lord. There is no sickness in Him. When God created our bodies and breathed the breath of life into us, He didn't breathe sickness into us. If we're sick, that sickness attached itself to our bodies as we strayed away from God and His ways. But God did not cause us to be sick. He is the One who heals us when we *do* get sick.

We know from Hebrews 13:8 that God is the same yesterday, today, and forever. So if God healed people in the Old Testament, like we read in the above verse, and if Jesus healed people in the New Testament, then we know the Lord can heal us today! He doesn't change. He is the same God who created the heavens and the earth, the same God who shed His blood on the cross at Calvary, and the same God who will touch and heal our bodies even today.

He is the same God who created the heavens and the earth, the same God who shed His blood on the cross at Calvary, and the same God who will touch and heal our bodies even today.

In this chapter, we will briefly explore how God healed people in the Old Testament, Jesus' healing ministry in the New Testament, the apostles' healing ministry, and the modern Church's healing ministry— that's you and me! God has the power to supernaturally heal people from any sickness they may be dealing with. And God is able to do the same for you and me. As we continue on in this chapter, we'll discover more about God's amazing supernatural power of healing.

Healing in the Old Testament

"And said, If thou wilt diligently hearken to the voice of the LORD thy God, and wilt do that which is right in his sight, and wilt give ear to his command-ments, and keep all his statutes, I will put none of these diseases upon thee, which I have brought upon the Egyptians: for I am the LORD that healeth thee" (Exodus 15:26).

In this passage, we read how God promised the Israelites that no disease was going to come upon them. But this was a conditional prom-ise, meaning God was going to fulfill it as long as the Israelites fulfilled the conditions He required. Even though this was directed to the Israel-ites, this promise applies to us as well. If we will fulfill the conditions mentioned in this passage, God will not allow any of the diseases that the Egyptians experienced to come upon us. In fact, He will heal us of any sicknesses we may be experiencing. But what are some of those conditions?

Well, we read in verse 26a, *"If thou wilt diligently hearken to the voice of the LORD thy God..."* So when we listen to the Word being preached or when we read the Word in our own devotionals, we are to do so attentively. But what's the purpose of listening carefully? Well, it says in verse 26b, *"and wilt do that which is right in his sight."* We are to listen diligently to the voice of God in order to do what is pleasing in His sight.

Then verse 26c describes what is pleasing in God's sight. It continues, *"...and wilt give ear to his commandments, and keep all his statutes..."* Those are the things that God finds pleasing. When we listen to, obey, and keep His commandments, we become pleasing to God. But it's impossible to obey God's commandments if we don't first hearken to His voice. That's why we have to keep our ears attuned to His voice and learn what is pleasing to Him. Then we are to take the Word and apply it to our lives through obedience to His commandments.

When we do that, we will receive the promise that we read in the last part of verse 26, where God says, *"I will put none of these diseases upon thee, which I have brought upon the Egyptians: for I am the LORD that healeth thee."* None of the diseases that the Egyptians experienced are going to come upon us, because we have hearkened to God's voice and have obeyed His commandments. But it's important to remember that this promise can only be ours once we have kept the conditions that God requires.

Wise Words Bring Healing

Another Old Testament passage about healing is found in Proverbs 4:20–22, where we read, *"My son, attend to my words; incline thine ear unto my sayings. Let them not depart from thine eyes; keep them in the midst of thine heart. For they are life unto those that find them, and health to all their flesh."* This is an interesting teaching about healing. According to these passages, when a son doesn't stray from the words of his father, those words will bring life and health to him. In this context, the word "life" means to be revived, lively, and flowing like fresh water.

It says in verse 22a that we are supposed to "find" the words, meaning we should try to discover the meaning of those words and prove them in our life experiences. Aside from putting them in our hearts, we have to practice those words. When we do, we'll experience life, and according to verse 22b, we'll experience health in our flesh. The flesh is the body. So we can see here in this Old Testament teaching on healing that the words of a father produce life and health in the body of his son when his son places those words in his heart and practices them in his life.

Wise people who use their words for good will create health in their lives and the lives of those who listen to them.

In Proverbs 12:18 we read, *"There is that speaketh like the piercings of a sword: but the tongue of the wise is health."* In this passage, we read that health is given to those who speak wisely. There are people who use their speech to stab like a sword, but there are others who use their words in a wise and prudent way to bless those around them. And those wise people who use their words for good will create health in their lives and the lives of those who listen to them. So not only do the father's words create life and health, but people who use their tongues with wisdom will also bring healing to their bodies and to those who listen to them.

Healing is connected to the spirit and healing comes through our words.

In Proverbs 13:17 we read, *"A wicked messenger falleth into mischief: but a faithful ambassador is health."* A faithful ambassador is someone who is trustworthy and honest. That person will bring health to himself and others.

Then, in Proverbs 15:4 it says, *"A wholesome tongue is a tree of life: but perverseness therein is a breach in the spirit."* A wholesome tongue represents a person who speaks healing. According to this passage, a person who speaks healing is like a tree of life, something that is fruitful. But the perverseness of a person is like a breach in the spirit, meaning perverseness violates the spirit. It's interesting to notice from this passage that healing is connected to the spirit and that healing comes through our words.

We read something similar in Proverbs 16:24: *"Pleasant words are as an honeycomb, sweet to the soul, and health to the bones."* Pleasant words are favourable words of kindness, goodness, and praise. When we speak encouraging words, those words are sweet to the soul, meaning they're acceptable to our inner being. Not only that, but those words will bring health to our bones. It's amazing how even in the Old Testament we read that our words have an effect on our physical well-being. It says in Psalm 107:20, *"He sent his word, and healed them, and delivered them from their destructions."*

Healing Comes After Conversion

Another element of healing in the Old Testament is found in Isaiah 6:10, where we read, *"Make the heart of this people fat, and make their ears heavy, and shut their eyes; lest they see with their eyes, and hear with their ears, and understand with their heart, and convert, and be healed."* What is important to understand about healing in this Old Testament passage is that healing is connected to conversion. Conversion means to turn back from our own ways, turn toward God, and start doing things that are pleasing to Him. In other words, healing is connected to the restoration of our relationship with God.

Imagine how our health can improve just by converting to God, coming back to Him, confessing our sins, and putting our trust and confidence in His Word.

When we convert to God, we get healed. Healing comes through repentance. As I said, a lot of our sicknesses come as a result of sin. So those sicknesses can be removed if we just convert to God, confess our sins, and allow Him to wash our sins away through the application of the shed blood of our Lord Jesus Christ.

Not only that, but we need to have trust and confidence in God.

Imagine how our health can improve just by converting to God, coming back to Him, confessing our sins, and putting our trust and confidence in His Word. Another Old Testament verse that confirms this is Isaiah 19:22b, where we read, *"They shall return even to the LORD, and he shall be intreated of them, and shall heal them."*

A very important Old Testament passage about healing is Isaiah 53:4–5, where we read, *"Surely he hath borne our griefs, and carried our sorrows: yet we did esteem him stricken, smitten of God, and afflicted. But he was wounded for our transgressions, he was bruised for our iniquities: the chastisement of our peace was upon him; and with his stripes we are healed."*

This is such a significant passage. Notice again that salvation from a life of sin is connected to the healing of our bodies. Jesus Christ bore our griefs and carried our sorrows. He was wounded for our transgressions and bruised for our iniquities, and with His stripes we are healed. Our healing has already happened on the cross at Calvary. The moment we receive salvation, we have the same power to receive healing. So if there are symptoms of sicknesses in our bodies, we have to go back to the sacrifice of the Lord Jesus Christ in order to be healed.

Health Comes When We Have a True Fast

Let's take a look at another Old Testament passage that, in my view, is very important for healing. In Isaiah 58:8 we read, *"Then shall thy light break forth as the morning, and thine health shall spring forth speedily: and thy righteousness shall go before thee; the glory of the LORD shall be thy reward."* In this chapter, God describes a true fast that is acceptable in His eyes. When you and I do what this fast requires of us, we will receive light, meaning we'll receive direction in our lives and our healing will come speedily.

This verse also says that the glory of the Lord will be our reward. There are several rewards mentioned in this context. One of them is found in verse 11, where we read, *"And the LORD shall guide thee continu-*

20

ally, and satisfy thy soul in drought, and make fat thy bones: and thou shalt be like a watered garden, and like a spring of water, whose waters fail not." God will bring healing in our body and bones when you and I have a true fast. Have you ever wondered what God considers a true fast?

Well, we read in Isaiah 58:6–7, *"Is not this the fast that I have chosen? to loose the bands of wickedness, to undo the heavy burdens, and to let the oppressed go free, and that ye break every yoke? Is it not to deal thy bread to the hungry, and that thou bring the poor that are cast out to thy house? when thou seest the naked, that thou cover him; and that thou hide not thyself from thine own flesh?"* In other words, healing, divine guidance in our lives, satisfaction in our hearts, and strength in our bones will come as a result of us doing something tangible for the hungry and the poor.

It says here that we are to divide our bread with the hungry. This doesn't mean we're supposed to share what is left over of our food but that which *we* would normally eat. That means cutting back on some personal expenses to help feed the hungry. That is what God considers a true fast. He wants us to give an offering to help the poor.

Frequently in the Old Testament, people gave an offering to God before they received healing from Him. A passage that confirms this is 1 Samuel 6:3, where we read, *"And they said, If ye send away the ark of the God of Israel, send it not empty; but in any wise return him a trespass offering: then ye shall be healed, and it shall be known to you why his hand is not removed from you."* In other words, God wanted the people to offer a sacrifice to Him so that they would be healed.

> *Healing, divine guidance in our lives, satisfaction in our lives, and strength of our bones will come as a result of us doing something tangible for the hungry and poor.*

God is the One who brings healing. We can see all through the Old Testament that God is the Healer. In Jeremiah 33:6 it says, *"Behold, I will bring it health and cure, and I will cure them, and will reveal unto them the abundance of peace and truth."* Only God brings health and cure.

God says that He will cure us, and He will reveal unto us the abundance of peace and truth. Peace here is *shalom*, which really indicates completeness in body, soul, and spirit. There should be nothing broken and nothing missing in your life. Truth here is faithfulness, sureness, and stability. In other words, not only is God the healer but He is also the One who gives us peace and truth. And it is exactly through His peace and truth that He heals us.

So we can see from these Old Testament passages (there are many, many more passages) that God is the One who heals and cures us. He heals and cures through a number of ways: our obedience, the words we speak, the words God speaks, our repentance from sin, and our sacrificial offering.

Now let us explore healing in the New Testament through Jesus' ministry.

Jesus' Healing Ministry

"How God anointed Jesus of Nazareth with the Holy Ghost and with power: who went about doing good, and healing all that were oppressed of the devil; for God was with him" (Acts 10:38).

God anointed Jesus with the Holy Spirit and power. That anointing allowed Jesus to heal all those who were oppressed by the devil. Every sick person who came to Jesus received healing. I've never read anywhere in the Bible that Jesus made anyone sick. He always made them well. Jesus' ministry was to preach the gospel and heal the sick.

It says in Matthew 4:23, *"And Jesus went about all Galilee, teaching in their synagogues, and preaching the gospel of the kingdom, and healing all manner of sickness and all manner of disease among the people."* It's interesting to notice that the first thing Jesus did was teach. The second thing He did was preach. Then, after teaching and preaching the gospel, He healed people of their sicknesses. That was the order He followed.

So not only was Jesus teaching about His healing power, He was also preaching about salvation through faith in Himself. Then He started healing people, curing them, and restoring them to perfect health. It's important for us to understand that any healing experience or healing ministry has to occur after the teaching and preaching of the Word.

We read something similar in Matthew 9:35: *"And Jesus went about all the cities and villages, teaching in their synagogues, and preaching the gospel of the kingdom, and healing every sickness and every disease among the people."* Again, Jesus was teaching and preaching first. After that, He healed every sickness and disease among the people.

It's also interesting to notice that Jesus healed *everyone.* Each and every person who came to Jesus got healed. He didn't leave anybody out. It doesn't matter what kind of disease it was, Jesus healed them all. In Matthew 11:5 it says, *"The blind receive their sight, and the lame walk, the lepers are cleansed, and the deaf hear, the dead are raised up, and the poor have the gospel preached to them."* Jesus healed people who dealt with all kinds of sicknesses. There was not a single sickness that Jesus couldn't heal. In fact, He even raised the dead.

Jesus Healed by Casting Out Spirits

In Matthew 8:16 we read, *"When the even was come, they brought unto him many that were possessed with devils: and he cast out the spirits with his word, and healed all that were sick."* There is so much said in these few words. This passage reveals such great truths about the power of Jesus. At the time, many people were brought to Jesus who were under the power of demons. So Jesus cast out the evil spirits and then healed the people. Why would the Word of God connect the act of casting out demons with the result of healing? Because the two are, in fact, connected.

> *There was not a single sickness that Jesus couldn't heal. In fact, He even raised the dead!*

As I discussed in Chapter One, some people may be sick as a consequence of their disobedience. Some people may be sick because they lack knowledge about the effects of an unhealthy lifestyle. Others are sick because of their wrongful confessions.

But sometimes people are sick because of an evil spirit, a spirit of sickness.

As I already said, the source of sickness is not God. Otherwise, Jesus, the Son of God, wouldn't have healed all those people who were sick. The source of sickness is Satan. That's why we read in the Gospels that many times when Jesus healed people, He would cast out an evil spirit first and then the person would be healed.

According to John 6:63, the words of Jesus are spirit and life. So if we can relate God's Spirit to the words of Jesus, we can understand that evil spirits are connected to the words of Satan. If the words of God are spirit and life, the words of Satan are spirit and death. With that understanding, we can conclude that evil spirits are in relation to satanic words. Satan's words are any words that are contrary to the Word of God. The moment we accept Satan's words and believe them as truth, we become oppressed with evil spirits, and we will receive exactly what those words entail.

Every single word we hear and speak is a spirit. Jesus said that His words are spirit and life (John 6:63). Therefore, our words are spirit as well. Whenever we listen to something, the words we hear are spirits. For example, if you listen to a song that does not glorify God but is perverse and ungodly, those lyrics will have an effect on your thinking and feeling. There are spirits behind those words. If you allow those spirits to enter your heart, you are going to be negatively influenced by those evil spirits.

However, the lyrics of good and godly music can cast out evil spirits as well. An example of this is found in the story of King Saul and David. When King Saul was being attacked by an evil spirit, he called upon David to play music for him. In 1 Samuel 16:23b we read, *"David took an harp, and played with his hand: so Saul was refreshed, and was well, and the evil spirit departed from him."* As soon as David started playing the harp, the evil spirit that was tormenting Saul departed. So in some cases music can be used in a positive way to bring about healing in our lives.

But if you listen to gossip or watch violent movies or perverse television shows, those things can bring a poisonous spirit into you and that spirit can destroy your body. If you let evil words come into your ears, enter your mind, and seep down into your heart, those evil words (which are actually evil spirits) will try to harm your well-being.

So at the time, people who were possessed and oppressed by evil spirits were coming to Jesus in need of healing. Jesus would heal those people by casting out the evil spirits that were attacking their bodies. Notice that He didn't physically whip the spirits out of the people. He didn't negotiate with the spirits. He didn't ask nicely for the spirits to go. He simply commanded them to go because He has all the authority and power to do so. It's important to understand that evil spirits have no power on the earth other than when they're in a body.

Evil spirits have no power on the earth other than when they're in a body.

In 1995, my daughter Sara was only five years old and my son David was three years old. One night, Sara was in her room sleeping and in the middle of the bedroom she saw a snake, a spirit. For a few days, she was living in fear. Around the same time, my son David, who was sleeping in his bedroom, saw a woman spirit sitting next to him on the bed, and he started developing fear. But neither of them shared this with me right away. It wasn't until days later that they finally shared this with me.

So I said, "Those are just spirits. They have no power over you because they have no authority on the earth other than when they're in a body. And they're not in our bodies because our bodies are the temple of the Holy Spirit. God has given us dominion over those evil spirits. So let's go into every room of our home, anoint those rooms with oil, declare that we are washed by the blood of Jesus, and command those spirits to leave in Jesus' name."

The children agreed and that's what we did. We went into every room of our house and commanded every evil spirit to leave our home in Jesus' name. After we did that, those spirits never came back again. God has given us power to command any evil spirit to leave our midst.

The only way an evil spirit can take possession of a body is if that person allows that spirit to control him or her. Some people leave themselves open for an evil spirit to take possession of their bodies by exposing themselves to ungodly and evil words. Some people even worship Satan, and that's an open door to demonic possession as well. As spirit-filled Christians, Satan cannot take possession of our bodies, because the Holy Spirit resides within us. Our bodies are the temple of God's Spirit. Since we're filled with the Spirit of God, we cannot become possessed by an evil spirit. But we can let the evil spirit oppress us, as mentioned above, if we let these evil words and thoughts percolate through our minds and hearts.

Jesus Healed by Giving a Command

In Mark 3:5b we read, *"He saith unto the man, Stretch forth thine hand. And he stretched it out: and his hand was restored whole as the other."* At the time, Jesus went into a synagogue where He saw a man with one withered hand; it had become withered because of an accident or disease (verse 1). This man's hand was completely useless. He couldn't do anything with it. So as he was sitting in the synagogue worshipping God on the Sabbath day, Jesus walked in.

Then, in verse 2, we read that the Pharisees kept a close eye on Jesus to see if He would heal the man on the Sabbath day. According to Jewish customs, the Sabbath day was the day of rest and these religious leaders were looking for an opportunity to accuse Jesus of working on the Sabbath.

Nobody likes accusations. It's very difficult to be accused of something, even if we've done wrong and the accusations are correct. But it's even *more* difficult to be accused of something when we've done *right*. Whenever Jesus was accused, He was always accused for doing right. In this case, the Pharisees wanted to accuse Jesus for healing someone on the Sabbath day.

When Jesus saw the man with the withered hand, He told him to stand up in the midst of everybody (verse 3). Whenever Jesus healed the sick, He wanted everyone around to see, because healing was evidence of divine power. Then we read, in verse 4a, that as Jesus brought the man to the middle of the synagogue, He looked at the people and said, *"Is it lawful to do good on the sabbath days, or to do evil? to save life, or to kill?"* The crowd didn't say anything (verse 4b).

So then, in verse 5b, we read that Jesus looked at the man with the withered hand and gave him a command. The command was, *"Stretch forth thine hand."* In other words, Jesus commanded the man to do something he couldn't do, something he could only do by the power of God. Being obedient to what God said made it possible for this man to stretch forth his hand. Then, in the last part of verse 5, it says, *"And he stretched it out: and his hand was restored whole as the other."*

It's interesting to notice that this was how Jesus healed the man. Whenever Jesus healed people, He always gave a command. I mentioned earlier that whenever Jesus would cast out the devil, He always commanded the devil to leave. He simply gave a command, and the devil had to obey.

You are to command things to happen in Jesus' name. Then you are to act in obedience to the Word of God.

Think back to the story of the ten lepers. God healed them when they acted based on what Jesus commanded them to do. In Luke 17:14 we read, *"And when he saw them, he said unto them, Go shew yourselves unto the priests. And it came to pass, that, as they went, they were cleansed."* They didn't receive their healing right there and then. They were healed when they went to show themselves to the priests (when they obeyed the command of Jesus).

So in Mark 3:5, Jesus gave the man with a withered hand a command to hold out his hand. Once the man obeyed, his hand was completely restored. He gained full use of his hand just as he had before. That man's obedience to the command of Jesus demonstrated that he believed he could be healed. That's why he acted in obedience. But if he'd had doubt in his heart, if he'd hesitated to hold out his hand, or if he'd refused to hold out his hand, he wouldn't have been healed.

When you are trusting God for a miracle in your life, you are to command things to happen in Jesus' name. Then you are to act in obedience to the Word of God. That's how you'll receive healing. But if you ask questions or doubt the Word of God, you are only stopping the miracle from taking place in your life. That's why you are to act in obedience and faith, just as this man with the withered hand did and just as the ten lepers did. Healing comes when you command it to come by faith in the name of Jesus Christ and when you embrace the commandments of God through obedience.

There are many more miracles that took place during Jesus' ministry. If we were to study each and every one of them, we would notice a similar pattern. First, we would notice that the manifestation of Jesus' healing power always included the teaching and preaching of the Good News. Secondly, we would notice that Jesus often healed people by casting out an evil spirit or giving a command. And thirdly, we would see that their healing, or lack of it, was based on their faith and obedience to God. That was the pattern that Jesus followed.

Now let's take a look at the apostles' ministry. As we do, we'll notice that the apostles followed a similar pattern in their own healing ministry.

The Apostles' Healing Ministry

"And when he had called unto him his twelve disciples, he gave them power against unclean spirits, to cast them out, and to heal all manner of sickness and all manner of disease" (Matthew 10:1).

Jesus gave all the apostles the same power He had. So just like Jesus, the apostles had the power of the Holy Spirit to lay hands on people, cast out demons, and heal the sick in Jesus' name. The apostles' ministry didn't start after Jesus ascended into heaven; it actually started when Jesus sent out the seventy. In Luke 10:1 we read, *"After these things the Lord appointed other seventy also, and sent them two and two before his face into every city and place, whither he himself would come."*

Everybody who came to the apostles to be healed had to have faith that they would receive their healing.

One of the first recorded incidents of healing in the apostles' ministry after Jesus went to heaven is found in Acts 3:16, where we read, *"And his name through faith in his name hath made this man strong."* This verse is referring to a man who could not walk but was healed because Peter spoke the word of healing to him.

Just like Jesus, the apostles healed people by speaking the Word. Not only did they speak the word of healing, they spoke in the name of Jesus. From this passage, we also see that faith played a major role in healing. In Jesus' healing ministry, faith had to be evident in the people who wanted to receive healing. The same was true during the apostles' healing ministry. Everybody who came to the apostles in need of healing had to have faith that they would be healed.

In Acts 5:16 we read, *"There came also a multitude out of the cities round about unto Jerusalem, bringing sick folks, and them which were vexed with unclean spirits: and they were healed every one."* In this verse, we find two similarities between Jesus' healing ministry and the apostles' healing ministry. The first similarity is that people were bringing those who were sick and vexed with unclean spirits to the apostles, just like they did with Jesus when He was on the earth. The second similarity is that every one of them got healed, just like everyone who came to Jesus got healed.

It says in Acts 14:9, *"The same heard Paul speak: who steadfastly beholding him, and perceiving that he had faith to be healed."* This passage is about a crippled man who was listening as the gospel was being preached. (So, like in Jesus' ministry, there had to be preaching of the gospel prior to healing.) Then, as the man was listening to the gospel, faith rose up in his heart and Paul could see that he believed he could be healed. So Paul commanded the man to stand up and the man jumped to his feet and was healed. (Again, a command had to be made before healing could take place.) This order of preaching and then healing is very similar to the order of Jesus' ministry.

We read in Acts 19:11–12, *"And God wrought special miracles by the hands of Paul: So that from his body were brought unto the sick handkerchiefs or aprons, and the diseases departed from them, and the evil spirits went out of them."* Think about the woman who had the issue of blood for twelve years (Matthew 9:20). She received her healing by touching the hem of Jesus' garment (Matthew 9:21). She didn't touch Jesus Himself, but His hem. Here we read something similar. We read that the apostle Paul healed people as they were touching the handkerchiefs or aprons that Paul was using.

There are many similarities between Jesus' healing ministry and the apostles' healing ministry. In John 14:12 Jesus said, *"Verily, verily, I say unto you, He that believeth on me, the works that I do shall he do also; and greater works than these shall he do; because I go unto my Father."* That's exactly what the apostles were doing. The same things that were happening during the time of Jesus were happening during the time of the apostles, except in greater quantity.

The Disciples' Lack of Faith

The apostles had a great healing ministry after Jesus ascended into heaven. However, their ministry didn't start out that way. While Jesus was on the earth, they had to learn from Him and gradually increase their faith as they saw Jesus practice the gift of healing. In Mark 9, we read a story that happened during the early

The choice to have faith in order to drive out demons in Jesus' name, to declare health over people in Jesus' name, and to perform signs and wonders in Jesus' name is ours to make.

stages of the disciples' ministry and how their lack of faith caused Jesus to rebuke them.

In Mark 9:19 it says, *"He answereth him, and saith, O faithless generation, how long shall I be with you? how long shall I suffer you? bring him unto me."* This was quite a rebuke that Jesus gave to His disciples. At the time, a man had brought his son to Jesus because his son had a dumb spirit (verse 17). This dumb spirit was tormenting his son and causing him to convulse, foam at the mouth, grind his teeth, fall into a motionless stupor, and waste away (verse 18). Originally, this man had asked the disciples to cast the dumb spirit out, but the disciples were unable to. So he brought his son before Jesus.

Then, in verse 19a, we read that Jesus rebuked His disciples. Jesus called them a *"faithless generation."* The reason they couldn't cast out the spirit was that they didn't have any faith. They were full of doubt and they questioned whether or not their prayers would work. As a result, their prayers *didn't* work.

Then, in verse 19b, Jesus said, *"How long shall I be with you?"* In the German translation, *Hoffnung fuer Alle*—which means, *Hope for All*—this part of the verse says, *"Wann wollt ihr endlich anfangen zu glauben?"* In English, this translates to, *"When are you finally going to begin believing?"* That was the disciples' key problem. They had not begun to believe in the power that Jesus had invested in them. Instead, they were trying to cast out this demon with their own strength.

Jesus was quite unhappy with the disciples because they had not begun to believe. The disciples' belief did not depend on Jesus; it depended on them. Faith is a choice. It is a frame of mind and of spirit completely tuned to the Word of God. The choice to have faith to drive out demons in Jesus' name, to declare health over people in Jesus' name, and to perform signs and wonders in Jesus' name is ours to make. God will not make that decision for us. He has already pronounced His Word and given us the power we need. Now we are the ones who have to choose to open our mouths with faith. The Word has been declared; now it's our job to believe that Word, and we are to speak it with our mouth with full confidence that what He has declared He will perform (Jeremiah 1:12). That's how miracles happen in our lives.

In Mark 9:25b, we read what Jesus did once the man brought his son before Him: *"He rebuked the foul spirit, saying unto him, Thou dumb and deaf spirit, I charge thee, come out of him, and enter no more into him."* In other words, Jesus commanded the deaf and dumb spirit to come out of the boy, and that's exactly what happened. In verses 26–27 we read, *"And the spirit cried, and rent him sore, and came out of him: and he was as one dead; insomuch that many said, He is dead. But Jesus took him by the hand, and lifted him up; and he arose."*

Now, there are some situations where more time is required before a miracle comes. In verse 29 we read, *"And he said unto them, This kind can come forth by nothing, but by prayer and fasting."* Sometimes we are required to keep persevering until the miracle takes place. In this case, the disciples needed to keep on praying and fasting. But instead of doing that, they gave up because they lacked faith.

Peter Heals a Crippled Man

It was after Jesus went to heaven that the apostles' ministry really expanded. Also at this point, they experienced the baptism of the Holy Spirit (Acts 2). After that, they had more faith and power to pray for people to be healed. One such example is found in Acts 3:16, where we read, *"And his name through faith in his name hath made this man strong, whom ye see and know: yea, the faith which is by him hath given him this perfect soundness in the presence of you all."*

According to verse 1, Peter and John were going to the temple to pray at about three o'clock in the afternoon. Then, in verse 2, it says that a certain man who was crippled since birth was being carried along. Every day, this man would lay at the gates to beg for money from those who were entering the temple. In verse 3, it says that when Peter and John were about to go into the temple, the man asked them for a gift. In verse 4, we read that both Peter and John gazed at the man and said,

"Look on us." According to verse 5, this crippled man thought Peter and John were going to give him money.

But in verse 6, Peter said, *"Silver and gold have I none; but such as I have give I thee: In the name of Jesus Christ of Nazareth rise up and walk."* Peter commanded this crippled man to walk. But notice that Peter didn't make this commandment in his own name, but in the name of the Lord Jesus Christ. It says in verse 7, *"And he took him by the right hand, and lifted him up: and immediately his feet and ankle bones received strength."* This crippled man became healed at the name of Jesus. Then, in verse 8, it says, *"And he leaping up stood, and walked, and entered with them into the temple, walking, and leaping, and praising God."*

So when people saw this miracle, they were astonished because they recognized this man as the same man who was crippled and always begging for alms (verse 9). It says in verse 10b that they *"were filled with wonder and amazement at that which had happened unto him."* So all the people came and crowded around Peter and John (verse 11). This was when Peter began preaching the gospel.

As he was preaching, he pointed out that Jesus Christ was glorified (verse 13), that He was pure, holy, just, and blameless (verse 14), and that He was the Source and Author of life whom God had raised from the dead (verse 15). Because Jesus was glorified so greatly, in verse 16 Peter said to the people, *"And his name through faith in his name hath made this man strong, whom ye see and know: yea, the faith which is by him hath given him this perfect soundness in the presence of you all."*

Peter wanted to emphasize that the Lord Jesus Christ, who is glorified, pure, holy, just and blameless, and who is the very source of life, is the same Jesus that God raised from the dead and who has all the power in heaven and earth. Because Jesus has the power, anyone who speaks the name of Jesus and has faith in His name will have the same kind of power that Jesus has. When Peter spoke the name of Jesus, this man was completely healed of all the infirmities in his body. But notice that healing came by the name of Jesus and also by faith in His name.

So when you speak, you are not to speak in your own name but in the name of Jesus. When you are speaking to a person who needs healing, remember to use the authority and power in the name of Jesus to command that person's body to be healed. You have the ability to speak that way because the same power that God

Because Jesus has the power, anyone who speaks the name of Jesus and has faith in His name will have the same kind of power that Jesus has.

used to raise Christ from the dead is within you (Romans 8:11). When you speak in the name of Jesus, you can perform all the miracles that Jesus did. Just like Peter, you have every authority to command your body or someone else's body to be healed when you speak in the name of Jesus.

Now that we've taken a glimpse at the healing ministry of the apostles, let's move on to discuss our healing ministry today. The miracles of healing weren't just for the disciples. They're for us as well. We have the same power and authority to pray for healing and may therefore expect that people will be healed. When we follow the example of Jesus and the apostles—when we do what they did—we'll see the same miracles that they saw.

Our Healing Ministry

"And these signs shall follow them that believe; in my name shall they cast out devils; they shall speak with new tongues; they shall take up serpents; and if they drink any deadly thing, it shall not hurt them; they shall lay hands on the sick, and they shall recover" (Mark 16:17–18).

Before Jesus ascended into glory, He gave us what's known as the Great Commission (Matthew 28:18–20). God has given us the power to do what He has commissioned us to do; otherwise, He wouldn't have given us this commission. The same power and spirit that raised Jesus from the dead is within us (Romans 8:11). Our healing ministry includes making use of the power that God has given us, which is actually the presence of God in our lives.

The words of Jesus spoken by His own lips had the power to heal. If the words of Jesus are upon our lips, they have no less power to heal than when they were on His lips. His words on His lips have the same power on our lips. So open your mouth and speak the words of healing over your body, over the bodies of your family, and over the bodies of other people for whom you are praying to be healed. In the same way Jesus and the apostles healed by the word of their mouths, we will receive healing by the word of our mouths.

> *The words of Jesus had the power to heal. If the words of Jesus are upon our lips, they have no less power to heal than when they were on His lips.*

The power to heal wasn't just given to the disciples, but to all believers. In fact, Jesus said in John 17:20, *"I am praying not only for these disciples but also for all who will ever believe in me because of their testimony"* (NLT). So if you and I are believers of God and His Word, in His name we have the power to cast out devils and heal the sick. We can command every evil spirit to leave our midst in Jesus' name. We are going to do whatever Jesus did and whatever the apostles did, and we're going to see the same results they saw.

In John 14:12 Jesus said, *"Verily, verily, I say unto you, He that believeth on me, the works that I do shall he do also; and greater works than these shall he do; because I go unto my Father."* The works that Jesus performed— such as preaching the gospel, healing the sick, and raising the dead— we're also going to perform, because Jesus is now in heaven with the Father. According to this verse, we're going to do those same works of Jesus, but in greater numbers. Now, in order to do that, we have to learn about the power of God within us.

In 1 Corinthians 12:8–11 we read: *"For to one is given by the Spirit the word of wisdom; to another the word of knowledge by the same Spirit; to another faith by the same Spirit; to another the gifts of healing by the same Spirit;*

to another the working of miracles; to another prophecy; to another discerning of spirits; to another divers kinds of tongues; to another the interpretation of tongues: But all these worketh that one and the selfsame Spirit, dividing to every man severally as he will."

There are nine gifts of the Spirit listed in these passages, and one of them is the gift of healing. That's the gift of laying hands on the sick, speaking healing into their lives, and having them experience perfect health.

The gift of healing was used more in the New Testament than in the Old Testament. That's not to say that it wasn't used in the Old Testament. We've quoted many Old Testament passages about healing. But it's used more in the New Testament. The gift of healing is also part of our healing ministry.

It's so important that we exercise this gift. We have to practice it. There's a saying that goes, *"Use it or lose it."* If we have a gift but we don't practice it, we may lose it. I studied auto mechanics in the early seventies because my mother

> *One of the longest journeys is the journey from the head to the heart, from knowing what the Word of God says about healing to truly believing in our hearts what the Word says. But the bridge between our head and our heart is our mouth.*

wanted me to finish a trade, and in that sense I am like one of the rabbis who also had to finish a trade prior to embarking on his theological studies. I've done the same. But I never worked in the field of mechanics after obtaining my license. I didn't really use the skills I learned. I know how to change a tire, but not much else. Because I didn't practice the skills I learned, I lost most of them. It's the same with the gift of healing. It's important that we exercise and practice that gift in our lives and the lives of others so that we don't lose it.

But in order to exercise the gift of healing, we need to have faith. Whenever Jesus or the apostles healed people, they spoke words of healing. When they spoke words of healing and the people who were sick believed those words, that's when healing came. So in order for us to see the manifestation of healing, we need to speak words of healing and then believe the words we've spoken.

One of the longest journeys is the journey from the head to the heart, from knowing what the Word of God says about healing to truly believing in our hearts what the Word says. But the bridge between our head and our heart is our mouth. When we open our mouths and speak words of healing, eventually those words will be buried in our hearts. Suddenly our faith will spring up, because our faith comes by hearing the Word of God (Romans 10:17). Then our faith, based on God's Word, will bring healing to our bodies or the bodies of whomever we're praying for.

So you and I have the power to command sicknesses to leave. It says in Isaiah 53:5b, *"With his stripes we are healed."* We read something similar in 1 Peter 2:24b, where it says, *"By whose stripes ye were healed."* The verse in 1 Peter 2:24b is written in the past tense, meaning you were already healed. Not only did God provide salvation for your soul, He also provided healing for your body. God wants you to be well. He doesn't want you to walk in sickness.

We read in James 5:16, *"Confess your faults one to another, and pray one for another, that ye may be healed. The effectual fervent prayer of a righteous man availeth much."* We need to confess our sins to one another, and then we need to pray for one another that we may be healed. In verse 14 we read, *"Is any sick among you? let him call for the elders of the church; and let them pray over him, anointing him with oil in the name of the Lord."* In verse 15 we read, *"And the prayer of faith shall save the sick, and the Lord shall raise him up; and if he have committed sins, they shall be forgiven him."* We can see that it's so important to pray with faith and conviction that whatever we pray for will come to pass.

So the same commands that Jesus gave to the apostles are given to us. We are to pray for the sick, lay hands on them, and heal them. That's exactly what Jesus did. That's exactly what the apostles did. And that's exactly what we're commanded to do. In other words, after Jesus went to heaven, His ministry was carried on through the apostles' ministry. Now that the apostles are gone, it's our job to carry on Jesus' ministry through *our* healing ministry. Jesus is alive and active through you and me today.

It's so interesting to study the Scriptures and learn about God's supernatural healing power in the lives of people in the Bible. By taking into consideration everything we learn about healing in the Old Testament and the healing ministries of Jesus and the apostles in the New Testament, we can really understand how our healing ministry should be conducted today. Now that we've discussed the nature of God's supernatural healing power—the healing that needs to be received by faith in our spirits—let's talk more specifically about how we can activate that power in our own lives through our soul.

In the following chapter, we'll take a look at the soul aspect of healing. One important aspect of how we receive healing is through our soul—by exercising our soul (our mind, will, and emotions) to do what's required to receive healing. We know that God has the ability to heal us supernaturally, but how exactly can we receive that supernatural healing? What do our souls need to do in order to experience God's supernatural healing in our lives? Let's proceed to Chapter Three and find out.

CHAPTER THREE
Soul: How to Receive God's Supernatural Healing

"Beloved, I wish above all things that thou mayest
prosper and be in health, even as thy soul prospereth"
(3 John 1:2).

Our soul's prosperity determines both the well-being of our health and the prosperity of every other area in our lives. In other words, the state of our physical health is based on our soul. But what does the soul consist of? The soul consists of the mind, emotions, and will. It's so important that our mind, emotions, and will be in harmony. How can we ensure they are in harmony? Well, we need to line up our thoughts, desires, and decisions with the Word of God.

When we line up what we think with the Word of God, our emotions will become influenced by our thoughts. After that, our will (our decisions) will be aligned with the will of God. So we harmonize our mind, emotions, and will by lining up our thoughts with God's Word. When we create the wellness of our soul, we will create an atmosphere

If you choose to make the Word of God the centre of your thoughts, ultimately your destiny will be determined by the Word.

for the wellness of our physical health and overall prosperity to take place.

It's interesting to notice that everything starts with a word. When we hear something, either when it is spoken to us or we say it to ourselves, that word has a tremendous influence on our lives. Words are some of the most powerful things God has given us. When a word enters our minds, it starts creating thoughts. If we continue to dwell on those thoughts, they eventually have an impact on our emotions. All of our emotions come as a result of the things we think about. For example, some people who hear a negative report from a doctor regarding their health start developing thoughts of fear. And because they dwell on those thoughts, they develop serious problems with depression. So our thoughts strongly influence our emotions.

Eventually our emotions will lead to our decisions. Most of the choices that we make are made because of a strong emotion that pushes us. Sometimes they can be good decisions; sometimes they can be bad decisions. For example, there are doctors who know all the negative effects of nicotine but still choose to smoke. Why? Their emotions push them to smoke. Our emotions have a huge amount of control over our decisions. They often take over our reasoning capacity.

When we make up our mind about something, that decision usually results in some sort of action related to our decision. And our continual actions create a habit in our lives. For example, a person who first learns to drive usually practices on a regular basis, paying attention to all the instructions he or she was given. But once that person masters the skill of driving, it becomes natural to him or her, and eventually that person starts driving with the habits he or she developed during the learning stages. The same habit formation happens with any repeated action we engage in.

Then our habits eventually determine our character. Whatever we continuously do, we become. For example, a person who habitually smokes cigarettes becomes a smoker. A person who habitually drinks alcohol becomes a drinker. Our habits establish our character. Finally, our character determines our destiny, which is where we end up.

Do you see how it all started with one word? That's why it's so important to allow the Word of God to be the preeminent word in our minds. We should think, meditate, and speak the Word of God day and night. Or, in other words, we should do so continually (Joshua 1:8). When we bury the Word of God in our hearts, it eventually becomes our thoughts, which in turn influences our emotions. Then our emotions motivate our decisions based on the Word, which should result in actions of obedience to God. Then our actions become habits, which determines our character and then leads us to our destiny. It really goes to show how powerful words are.

According to the *Hoffnung fuer Alle* German translation, Jesus said in Matthew 12:37, *"An euern Worten entscheidet sich eure Zukunft."* In English, this translates to, *"Upon your words, your destiny is determined."* If you choose to make the Word of God the centre of your thoughts, ultimately your destiny will be determined by the Word.

Forgiveness Comes Before Healing

"Confess your faults one to another, and pray one for another, that ye may be healed" (James 5:16a).

Sometimes, in a church setting, there are people who are sick. According to verse 14, in such cases a sick person should *"call for the elders of the church; and let them pray over him, anointing him with oil in the name of the Lord."* Then it says in verse 15 that *"the prayer of faith shall save the sick, and the Lord shall raise him up; and if he have committed sins, they shall be forgiven him."* It's interesting to notice that God connects healing with forgiveness. Before you can receive healing, you first need to receive God's forgiveness.

If you want to experience divine healing in your body, you need God's forgiveness first.

41

In Mark 2:5, 11b we read, *"When Jesus saw their faith, he said unto the sick of the palsy, Son, thy sins be forgiven thee... Arise, and take up thy bed, and go thy way into thine house."* This is a story about a paraplegic man who had four friends who wanted him to get healed. They broke a hole through the roof of the house that Jesus was preaching in and lowered a bed that the paraplegic man was lying on so that Jesus could heal him. When Jesus saw the faith of the four friends, He forgave the paraplegic man of his sins and then healed him. But notice the sequence: before Jesus healed him, He first forgave the man's sins.

If you want to experience divine healing in your body, you need God's forgiveness first. Healing and forgiveness are very closely connected to each other. Since some sicknesses are caused by sinful acts (as I discussed in Chapter One), you need to reconcile with God first by confessing your sins to Him and repenting from them. We read in 1 John 1:9, *"If we confess our sins, he is faithful and just to forgive us our sins, and to cleanse us from all unrighteousness."*

According to James 5:16a, if you are sick, the first thing you need to do is *"confess your faults one to another."* To confess your sins means to agree with God that you have done something wrong, something that is contrary to the will of God. When you confess your sins, you are openly acknowledging that you have committed a misdeed. Then, according to verse 16b, you are to *"pray one for another, that ye may be healed."* God doesn't want you to be sick. He wants you to pray and believe that you will be healed.

So the first step is confessing your sins, which is coming into agreement with God about your wrongful actions. Once you have agreed with God about your sins, you have to agree with Him about what He says concerning your healing.

What does God say about healing? Well, in Isaiah 53:5 we read, *"But he was wounded for our transgressions, he was bruised for our iniquities: the chastisement of our peace was upon him; and with his stripes we are healed."* Because Jesus shed His blood on the cross of Calvary, you have received forgiveness for your sins. Through that forgiveness, you have complete access to healing. But it's important to remember that forgiveness always comes before healing. If we don't take that forgiveness by faith, we will start to have a guilty conscience, which is very destructive to our immune system.

King Hezekiah's Healing

In Isaiah 38:16–17 we read, *"O Lord, by these things men live, and in all these things is the life of my spirit: so wilt thou recover me, and make me to live. Behold, for peace I had great bitterness: but thou hast in love to my soul delivered it from the pit of corruption: for thou hast cast all my sins behind thy back."* This was a prayer that King Hezekiah lifted up to God. In this chapter, we read that Hezekiah became very sick at the age of thirty-nine. According to verse 1a, he was so sick that he was supposed to die.

But in verse 16a, Hezekiah acknowledges that he lives on the words and deeds of God. Just like Hezekiah, we too live on the words and deeds of God. In fact, Jesus said in Matthew 4:4, *"Man shall not live by bread alone, but by every word that proceedeth out of the mouth of God."* People often forget that they live because of God. But it's so important to remember that God holds our lives in the palm of His hand.

You shouldn't work against what God says. You should work in line with what God

In verse 16b, Hezekiah asked God to heal him, to restore him to health again. Only God was able to restore him to perfect health. But notice what Hezekiah said in verse 17b: *"For thou hast cast all my sins behind thy back."* So we can see that God had already forgiven Hezekiah of his sins. That's why Hezekiah could now ask for healing.

According to Psalm 103:3, God is the one *"who forgiveth all thine iniquities; who healeth all thy diseases."* Committing iniquities means doing things that are contrary to the Word of God's clear commandments. Here it says that God forgives all of our iniquities. Not only does God forgive us of our sins, He also heals us of all our diseases. But we have to remember that forgiveness always comes before healing. We must first confess our sins before we can receive healing. We will experience God's healing touch after we experience His merciful forgiveness.

In Isaiah 6:10c we read, *"Convert, and be healed."* If you have turned away from God and have gone your own way, God instructs you here to stop doing what you have been doing and turn back to Him. You shouldn't work against what God says. You should work in line with what God says. According to this passage, healing will come when you convert back to Him. As I already mentioned, sometimes sicknesses are a result of disobedience. But God says here that you can be healed if you turn toward Him.

Do You Walk in Love?

In Mark 11:25-26 it says, *"And when ye stand praying, forgive, if ye have ought against any: that your Father also which is in heaven may forgive you your trespasses. But if ye do not forgive, neither will your Father which is in heaven forgive your trespasses."* Not only do you need God's forgiveness for your sins, but you also have to forgive those who have sinned against you.

You should never carry grudges in your heart. When you carry grudges in your heart, it's like drinking a cup of poison and thinking that the other person is going to die from it. If you hold a grudge in your heart, you're only hurting yourself. So you need to forgive others who have sinned against you. Then God will forgive you.

I heard of a mother who had a little girl who suffered from seizures. She was a lady of great means, so she had the money to get all the best medical help she could find in North America. But even though she got the best medical assistance, her daughter's seizures diminished only a little bit with the help of

Not only do you need God's forgiveness for your sins, but you also have to forgive those who have sinned against you.

medication. So she went to her pastor and asked him to pray for her daughter to be healed.

But rather than praying for her, the well-known pastor said, "Do you walk in love? Is there anyone in your heart that you don't love?"

The lady thought for a moment and said, "Yeah, my mother-in-law. I don't like her very much."

So the pastor said, "I'm not going to pray for your daughter." He told her that she needed to restore the relationship with her mother-in-law and walk in complete love first. So the lady listened to her pastor and restored her relationship with her mother-in-law.

Then she called her pastor and asked him to pray for her daughter now that the relationship with her mother-in-law had been restored. But the pastor said, "I'm not going to pray for her."

"Why not?" she asked him.

"I don't need to pray for her now," he answered. "Because you're walking in love, your daughter is already being healed." Sure enough, that's exactly what happened.

So we can see that healing comes after forgiveness, whether it is receiving it or granting it. If you are sick in your body and need a healing touch from the Lord, before praying for your healing first pray for forgiveness for anything that you may have done that was contrary to God's Word. Then search your heart to make sure you are walking in love. Forgive anyone who may have sinned against you. Then God will forgive you and heal you of your sickness.

According to German experts, bitterness and resentment can cause Post-Traumatic Embitterment Disorder (PTED). In an article of TopNews Health we read, "While Post-Traumatic Stress Disorder can be brought on by a serious accident or brutal crime or loss of a loved one, Post-Traumatic Embitterment Disorder can be the result of seething bitterness and resentment which builds up on a daily basis over a long period of time, according to the team of Berlin psychotherapists."[2]

The team was led by Dr. Michael Linden, who is the head of the psychiatric clinic at the Free University of Berlin (Freie Universität Berlin). They reported their findings in a journal of Psychotherapy and Psychosomatics. According to them, PTED is a reaction to a severe negative—usually relational—event, which can cause anger and resentment and bitter feelings. If that anger, resentment, and bitterness is not resolved it can cause all kinds of serious health issues like depression, insomnia, emotional instability, and outbursts of rage. Living in such a prolonged state with these kinds of negative feelings can cause stress, exacerbate cardiovascular problems, and reduce people's self-confidence and trust in others, which could eventually lead them to refuse socialization and ultimately become isolated. They develop a mentality of being a victim. PTED is different than PTSD (Post-Traumatic Stress Disorder), which is usually brought on by a serious accident or brutal crime or loss of a loved one, and PTED is usually a reaction to a severe negative relational event.[3]

Perfect Love Casts Out All Fear

One day, as I was preaching in Buffalo, New York, I went with the local pastor to a man's house to counsel him. He was about sixty-nine years old. Both he and his wife were Jewish believers, but he was very worried about dying. He was so worried that he became fearful of death. Whenever he would try to sleep, fearful thoughts would come into his mind. Those fears would cause his blood pressure to shoot up so high that they had to call an ambulance to the house on many occasions. This man lived in constant fear of dying.

I asked him, "Why are you so afraid?"

"Well, in my retirement building, a lot of people have died recently," he said. "I'm afraid that I'm going to die next."

I read to him 1 John 4:18: *"There is no fear in love; but perfect love casteth out fear: because fear hath torment. He that feareth is not made perfect in love."*

When you have perfect love, that love will cast out any fears you may have.

When you have perfect love, that love will cast out any fears you may have. There is no dread, no terror, and no fear when there is *agape* love, unconditional love that never ends. When you are perfected in that love, that love casts out all fear.

Based on that verse, I suspected that there was somebody in this man's life that he didn't love. I asked him, "Are you perfect in love? Is there anyone in your life that you don't love?"

He thought for a moment and said, "No, I like everybody. Maybe some people don't like me, but I like everybody."

I continued talking to him and said, "Did that fear of death come because you read the Word, and God's Word said that you were going to die?"

He answered, "No, of course not."

So then I said, "If your fear didn't come from God, then it must have come from Satan, the father of lies."

As we continued talking and I continued to encourage him, I asked him again, "Is there somebody in your life that you don't love?" It wasn't long before he confessed that he didn't like his son-in-law.

"My son-in-law has abused my daughter," he said. "I don't want him to be around my daughter. I don't want him to see his children, and I don't want him to see me."

"I agree with you that what your son-in-law did to your daughter is wrong," I said. "But your resentment toward your son-in-law is hurting your health. Because you're not perfect in love, that welcomes fear into your life. In this case, it's the fear of death."

I continued to counsel him and encouraged him to forgive his son-in-law and restore that relationship in Jesus' name. I led him in a prayer of confession, and in that prayer he forgave his son-in-law and asked God to remove the fear of death from his heart. After that, this man became joyful and happy again. There was a total change in his demeanour. His eyes were brighter and he was smiling. The reason he became so happy was that God had delivered him from that fear, which was caused by a lack of love in his life.

We can see from both biblical and current examples that forgiveness of sins is so important if we are to receive healing. There is no way you can receive healing from God if there is a sin between you and God. And there is no way you can receive the forgiveness of God if you haven't forgiven those who have wronged you (Mark 11:25–26).

For that reason, it's important that you reconcile your relationship with God if you know there's sin in your life. And an important part of receiving God's forgiveness is making sure you first forgive those who have sinned against you. This is absolutely essential if you want to receive healing.

Healing Comes Through the Word

"He sent his word, and healed them, and delivered them from their destructions" (Psalm 107:20).

Not only does healing come after forgiveness, but healing comes through the Word of God. According to the above passage, God sends His Word and heals people. God has done that in the past and He's doing it today. The Word of God is a form of medicine. There is no healing without the Word of God, and there is no deliverance without the Word of God. The Word in itself has the power to transform our lives. It is the seed of God that produces after its kind. For example, a plum seed produces a plum tree. A tomato seed produces a tomato plant. The seed of the Word of God produces exactly what the Word promises.

If you are troubled by something and nothing can help you, you know you have to go to the Word. When you are troubled, don't confess your situation or what other people are saying about your situation. Instead, confess the specific promise from the Word of God about that situation. When God sends His Word, He will bring about healing in your life (Psalm 107:20).

The moment you start believing that God will heal you personally is the moment you will receive your healing.

Whatever your trouble is, the word that God speaks will become a *rhema* word to you, meaning it will become a word that is directly to your spirit for your personal situation. A *rhema* word spoken to you is not a word that has been spoken to someone else. A *rhema* word is a Word of God that has been spoken to you specifically and that has been quickened within your heart. That's when your faith will be triggered into action. When you begin acting in faith, that's when healing and deliverance will come. The moment you start believing that God will heal you personally is the moment you will receive your healing.

One significant thing to notice is that God creates through His Word. He spoke a word and He created the heavens and earth. The term that is used to describe this is *ex nihilo*, a Latin word that means "out of nothing." God spoke a word and whatever He spoke came into existence. That's what we need to do as well. We need to speak ahead of time what we want to happen. Before we even see the manifestation of healing, we need to speak it. When we speak healing in the name of Jesus, we will be able to receive it.

Keep in mind that this is not the idea of "name it and claim it." There are so many things that need to happen from the point of naming it to the point of claiming it. There are actions that need to take place in order for us to have what we speak. We need to do our part to receive our healing, which I will discuss in the next chapter.

We Receive Healing the Same Way We Receive Salvation

When we first heard the gospel of Jesus Christ being preached, we received it in our hearts and we prayed the sinner's prayer. That's how we became saved. We heard the word of salvation, believed the word, confessed the word, and as a result we received what we had confessed, which was eternal salvation. Now we are new creatures in Christ Jesus. The Bible says that if you confess with your mouth and believe with your heart that Jesus is Lord and that He rose from the dead, you are saved (Romans 10:9). Since salvation comes through believing and confessing, healing will come by believing and confessing as well.

Why did we get saved but certain people didn't? Well, we read in Hebrews 4:2, *"For unto us was the gospel preached, as well as unto them: but the word preached did not profit them, not being mixed with faith in them that heard it."* The reason we got saved while others didn't was that we mingled or mixed the Word of God with faith.

In other words, we put our trust, reliance, and dependence upon that which we heard about salvation, and we were saved. We received the forgiveness of our sins. We have been born through the incorruptible seed of God, which is the Word of God (1 Peter 1:23). Salvation happened by hearing someone preach the Word. In Romans 10:17 we read, *"So then faith cometh by hearing, and hearing by the word of God."* When we heard the gospel, faith came into our hearts and we were saved.

The same process it took to receive salvation is the process needed to receive healing. We receive healing through the Word of God. There are many Bible verses about healing. When we take the word of healing and we believe it and confess it (just like we did with the word of salvation), we will be healed.

God wants everybody to get saved. He doesn't want anybody to perish. But not everyone accepts Him. Only those who accept Him will get saved. Now, equally so, God wants everybody to be healed. God doesn't want anybody to live in sickness. But not everyone gets healed because not everyone believes God's Word about healing.

In Matthew 6:10 we read, *"Thy kingdom come. Thy will be done in earth, as it is in heaven."* Jesus told us to pray that the will of God in heaven be done on the earth. As far as I know from the book of Revelation, there is no sickness in heaven. There's only complete

When we take the word of healing and we believe it and confess it (just like we did with the word of salvation), we will be healed.

health. So if we are to pray that God's will be on the earth as it is in heaven, we are to pray for things to be completely healthy on the earth.

In James 5:14 we read, *"Is any sick among you? let him call for the elders of the church; and let them pray over him, anointing him with oil in the name of the Lord."* God would not have asked us to be healed if He wanted us to be sick. In addition, God would never tell us to ask for something if it were not possible. God is instructing us to ask for healing because He wants to and is able to heal us. The same way we trust Him for our salvation, we need to trust Him for our healing.

As a Christian, if you fall into sin, what do you do to receive forgiveness? All you have to do is confess your sins to God and He is faithful and just to forgive you of your sins and cleanse you from all unrighteousness (1 John 1:9). When you and I confess our sins to God, forgiveness is not dependent on how good we are but on how good God is. It is because of *His* faithfulness and because of *His* justice that our sins will be forgiven. So when we confess, God's business is to forgive. All we need to do to receive God's forgiveness is hear the Word, believe the Word, and confess the Word. That's the same way we receive our healing.

It says in Isaiah 53:5b, *"With his stripes we are healed."* We read something similar in 1 Peter 2:24b, where it says, *"By whose stripes ye were healed."* These verses are words of healing. If we want to experience healing, we need to hear the word of healing, believe the word of healing, and confess the word of healing. Then we will be healed.

The Word of Healing is a Seed: Plant it in Your Heart

How do you get rid of a sickness? One way (the best way) is to simply believe that which God says in His Word. Now, don't misunderstand me. I do accept medical science. But medication can never cure a sickness. Medication is only there to control and stop the spread of a sickness. The same can be said about various types of surgeries. I'm not saying you shouldn't take the medical advice you receive from a doctor.[4] I believe God has given wisdom to doctors to help people. But I also believe in supernatural healing.

When you take the Word of God and confess it, those words become seeds planted into your spirit. When they're planted in your spirit, they have to be nurtured through prayer, meditation, and speaking. You have to let them grow and then, as Hebrews 4:2 says, you have to mix the Word of God with your faith. Think of a tomato seed, for example. When a tomato seed is still in its seed form, where is the tomato fruit? The fruit is inside the seed. So when you plant the seed, water it, and take care of it, God gives the sunlight and you receive your increase, which is the tomato.

According to Matthew 13, the Word of God is a seed. So the Word of God regarding healing is a seed that you need to plant. The fruit of that seed (the healing of your body) is already contained within that seed (the Word). What you need to do is plant that Word in your heart, confess it, believe it, and let your faith grow. Eventually, that seed will produce the fruit of your healed body.

> *The Word of God regarding healing is a seed that you need to plant. The fruit of that seed (the healing of your body) is already contained within that seed (the Word).*

Let's think back to the story about the woman with the issue of blood (Matthew 9:20–22). For twelve years, she went from one doctor to another, but not one of them could help her. Then she heard that Jesus could heal (Mark 5:27). Someone must have told her that Jesus was the Healer. Those words must have gone from her ears to her heart. She must have embraced and accepted those words, because they began to come from her heart out through her mouth.

We read in Matthew 9:21, *"For she said within herself, If I may but touch his garment, I shall be whole."* She didn't say, "I'm going to give this preacher a try. Maybe I'll get healed. Maybe I won't." Rather, she said,

"If I touch His hem, I *shall* be healed." She was speaking words of faith based on the word that she heard.

The garment Jesus was wearing was a prayer shawl.[5] At the bottom of the shawl were tassels (the hem of His garment). In the Hebrew culture, those tassels represented the commandments of God. So really, this woman was saying that if she just touched the tassels of Jesus' prayer shawl—meaning, if she just grabbed onto the Word of God—she would be healed.

In the Amplified Bible, Matthew 9:21 reads, *"For she kept saying to herself, If I only touch His garment, I shall be restored to health"* (AMP). Notice that the verb "kept saying" is given in present participle form, which represents a continuous action. She persistently said that if she touched the hem of Jesus' garment she would be healed. Because of her continual confession and her faith in the Word of healing, the moment she touched Jesus she did in fact receive her healing. At the time, there were many people touching Jesus, but only she was healed. Why? In verse 22b Jesus said, *"Daughter, be of good comfort; thy faith hath made thee whole."* Her faith mixed with the words of healing allowed her to receive her healing.

We know that Jesus is the Healer, but we also know that God could not have healed this woman if she hadn't believed in her heart, confessed with her mouth, and stretched out her hand to touch the garment of Jesus. If she had not done what she needed to do in order to be healed, she would not have been healed.

God will not provide healing for us if we don't stretch out and reach for it. Many people were touching Jesus at the time, but only this one woman got healed. She did what she was supposed to do: believe, confess, and act upon that confession of the Word of God. There is always something we have to do if we want to receive something from God. So because this woman confessed that she would be healed, believed that she would be healed, and reached out by faith, she was healed instantly.

It's amazing how much power our words have. According to Proverbs 18:21, *"Death and life are in the power of the tongue: and they that love it shall eat the fruit thereof."* You can determine whether you receive life or death in your situations just by the words that you speak.

When you hear the message that God sends His Word and heals you (Psalm 107:20), you need to confess that Word and believe it. Then you need to reach out by faith and God will heal you. I'm not talking about the power of positive thinking here. I'm talking about standing firm on the living Word of God regarding His promise to heal you and then walking in obedience to that Word.

The Word Needs to Shape You

"And be not conformed to this world: but be ye transformed by the renewing of your mind, that ye may prove what is that good, and acceptable, and perfect, will of God" (Romans 12:2).

Now that you are saved, your goals should be to become more Christ-like by the renewal of your mind and to please God by living in the new nature that God provides. You are to use the Word of God to transform yourself more into the image of Christ. In other words, your life, the words you say, and the actions you take should be completely directed by the Word of God. You shouldn't make any decisions in life unless they are Word-based decisions. That's why you need to *"let the Word of Christ dwell in you richly"* (Colossians 3:16). You were birthed from the Word. So the Word is the basis of explaining your past, present, and future.

God wants to shape you and your heart through the Word of God. God's Word should shape your future. So you need to allow the Word to reside within your mind. Once you do that, you have to choose with a willing heart to walk according to the Word. Then, once you use your will to make that decision, your emotions become the propelling force that moves you to that action. As you act upon the Word of God, you will live in harmony with the will of God. God's Word is His will. When you are in harmony with God's will, you will receive all the blessings of God, including the blessing of good health.

We read in 2 Corinthians 10:4–5, *"For the weapons of our warfare are not carnal, but mighty through God to the pulling down of strong holds; casting down imaginations, and every high thing that exalteth itself against the knowledge of God, and bringing into captivity every thought to the obedience of Christ."* The warfare that we are in is not a physical war but a spiritual one. That's why

> *A stronghold is an opinion or a belief system that strongly holds a person to something that is contrary to the will of God.*

Paul says here that the weapons of our warfare are not physical, meaning they're not made of flesh and blood. These weapons are spiritual and mighty before God.

But what are these weapons? Well, our most powerful weapon is the Word of God! God has given us His Word, which is *"sharper than any twoedged sword"* (Hebrews 4:12). The words that God speaks are our weapons of warfare.

Now, what are these weapons for? Well, verse 4b says that they're for *"the pulling down of strong holds."* A stronghold is an opinion or a belief system that strongly holds a person to something that is contrary to the will of God.

When something that is contrary to the Word of God comes into our minds and dwells there, it becomes a stronghold that keeps us from reaching our full potential in Christ. That stronghold needs to be broken. It doesn't matter what the imagination or thought is. If it is against

> *The Word of God within your heart is one of the major secrets the Lord uses to heal you.*

or above the knowledge of God, we are to bring those thoughts under the subjection of the lordship of Jesus Christ. Christ and His Word should rule supremely. That's what it means to renew our minds in the Word of God. God's Word, which is your weapon, has been given to you so that you will bring every thought under the lordship of Jesus Christ and defeat every stronghold that tries to exalt itself against the knowledge of

God. The Word of God within your heart is one of the major secrets the Lord uses to heal you.

Just recently, my wife and I were visiting a couple. The husband, who was a non-Christian, had cancer. His wife was a Christian. She was sharing with us that she heard in her church that maybe it was God's will for her husband to be sick.

"Okay, show me where in the Bible we read that God wants your husband to be sick," I said to her.

"I can't find it in the Bible," she responded. "But that's what people at my church told me."

So I read some Scriptures to her about God's desire to bring healing to our bodies. As I was reading, I could see that her non-Christian husband was becoming more and more interested in the Word of God. He wanted to hear the Word. He wanted to be prayed for. He wanted to receive God's healing touch. The seed that I was sowing was falling on good soil.

Faith comes by hearing, but fear comes by hearing, too. If you speak words of fear and sickness, you will hear them and believe them.

God wants you to stand on His Word regarding your healing. The Word of God within your heart is one of the major secrets the Lord uses to heal you. Declare that by the stripes of Jesus, you are healed (Isaiah 53:5). But let's say you do that and your symptoms continue.

And let's say you start confessing, "Oh, maybe that didn't work. Maybe I'm supposed to be sick." Those destructive words become weeds that will destroy what you confessed earlier about healing. Faith comes by hearing, but fear comes by hearing, too. If you speak words of fear and sickness, you will hear them and believe them. If you believe them, you will receive them.

So exclude every other word except the Word of God. Speak what God speaks about you. Don't speak what you feel or think, especially if it is contrary to the Word of God. Don't speak what other people are speaking. If it is not in line with the Word of God, do not accept it. Instead, speak and base your faith on what God says in His Word and you will be healed. God is not a liar. He will do exactly what He has promised. He will make you well.

Laying On of Hands

"And besought him greatly, saying, My little daughter lieth at the point of death: I pray thee, come and lay thy hands on her, that she may be healed; and she shall live" (Mark 5:23).

Throughout the New Testament, we read that Jesus and the disciples laid hands on the sick and the sick recovered. Sometimes, in order to get healed, you need a physical touch—for example, another person laying hands on you and praying for healing. As we lay hands on people, that human touch motivates and inspires faith in them. Then they get the results of what they're stretching their faith for, which is healing.

If the sick person were to lay hands on himself or herself and speak healing in a particular area, that would work as well. But sometimes another human touch is necessary. Some people need to receive the touch of another person in order to inspire their faith.

There was a study done involving two groups of patients to show the effects of human touch. When a doctor was visiting one group of patients, one person at a time, he purposely touched the patients as he was visiting them. When the doctor visited the second group of patients, he purposely refrained from touching them as he was visiting them.

All the patients received the same amount of time and attention from the doctor. But the study showed that those patients who were physically touched felt the doctor was more caring and that his diagnosis and treatment were more effective than those patients who were not physically touched. "The latest research indicates that neurons actually respond positively to human touch in anxiety-evoking situations. The researchers saw positive proof on an MRI of how dramatically human touch can even blunt physical pain and the anticipation of it."[6]

In Hebrews 6:1–2 we read, *"Therefore leaving the principles of the doctrine of Christ, let us go on unto perfection; not laying again the foundation of repentance from dead works, and of faith toward God, of the doctrine of baptisms, and of laying on of hands, and of resurrection of the dead, and of eternal judgment."*

This passage lists six fundamental principles of the Lord Jesus Christ's teachings. The first one is repentance, which leads to becoming born again. The second one is faith directed toward God. The third is the teaching about baptism. Then the fourth is the laying on of hands. The fifth is the resurrection of the dead, and the sixth is eternal judgment.

The laying on of hands was something that was practiced in the Old Testament as well as the New Testament. In Deuteronomy 34:9a we read, *"And Joshua the son of Nun was full of the spirit of wisdom; for Moses had laid his hands upon him."* Joshua received the same spirit of wisdom that Moses had because Moses laid his hands upon Joshua. This implies that whatever Moses had was transferred to Joshua through the laying on of hands.

In the New Testament, we read about God's power being transmitted from one person to another by faith through the laying on of hands. In Acts 13:3 we read, *"And when they had fasted and prayed, and laid their hands on them, they sent them away."* The apostles laid their hands on Barnabas and Saul before they sent them on their ministry trip. Also, we read in Acts 19:6, *"And when Paul had laid his hands upon them, the Holy Ghost came on them; and they spake with tongues, and prophesied."* When Paul laid hands on the Samaritan converts, they immediately received the Holy Spirit.

God heals through the laying on of hands.

Not only does laying hands on someone transmit power to that person, it can also bring healing. In Matthew 8:15 it says, *"And he touched her hand, and the fever left her: and she arose, and ministered unto them."* At the time, Peter's mother-in-law was sick with a fever. But all Jesus had to do was touch her and she was instantly healed. The touch of Jesus brought healing. In Mark 6:5b we read, *"He laid his hands upon a few sick folk, and healed them."* We can see throughout the Gospels that many times Jesus healed people by laying His hands upon them.

In Mark 8:22–25 we read a story about a blind man who came to Jesus and was healed. In verse 25 it says, *"After that he put his hands again upon his eyes, and made him look up: and he was restored, and saw every man clearly."* The blind man was healed when Jesus put His hands upon his eyes. In Acts 19:11 it says, *"And God wrought special miracles by the hands of Paul."* People who were sick became healthy again through the hands of Paul.

So, from these passages we can see that it's biblical to lay hands on the sick. But it's also important, when you're laying hands on people, that you believe God will heal them. Without faith, the act of laying hands on someone is just a ritual that will produce no results.

In Mark 5:22–23 we read, *"And, behold, there cometh one of the rulers of the synagogue, Jairus by name; and when he saw him, he fell at his feet, and besought him greatly, saying, My little daughter lieth at the point of death: I pray thee, come and lay thy hands on her, that she may be healed; and she shall live."* This man didn't just ask for prayer; he specifically asked Jesus to lay hands on his daughter. He had faith that if Jesus would touch his daughter, she would be healed. It's so important to incorporate faith with the act of laying hands.

It's important that we lay hands on people when we pray for healing. God heals through the laying on of hands. In Mark 16:17–18 we read, *"And these signs shall follow them that believe; in my name shall they cast out devils; they shall speak with new tongues; they shall take up serpents; and if they drink any deadly thing, it shall not hurt them; they shall lay hands on the sick, and they shall recover."* The act of laying hands on people is something that we ought to practice. It's a way Jesus healed people. It's a way the apostles healed people, and it's a way we today can practice the gift of healing.

GOD'S HEALING SECRETS

Prayer and Faith

"Therefore I say unto you, What things soever ye desire, when ye pray, believe that ye receive them, and ye shall have them" (Mark 11:24).

This passage is about prayer and faith. In verse 22 it says, *"And Jesus answering saith unto them, Have faith in God."* So the first thing your faith should be directed toward is God. Then, in verse 23, Jesus taught about speaking to the mountain and commanding it to be thrown into the sea. He said that if you believe what you have spoken, it will be done for you. So according to verse 23, your faith should be directed toward your words.

The third area that your faith should be directed toward is prayer (which we read in verse 24). As you pray for things, you have to believe that what you've prayed for has already been granted to you. The same can be said about my own mother. If she promised me something, I knew in my heart that it was done. I raised my children the same way. I always keep my promises to them. That is why I don't make too many promises. But once I make them, they are assured it is the same as done. And it always is.

God wants us to take it by faith as though we already have it by the time He promises it to us. Like with our natural parents and children, it might take time from the time of the promise until the physical manifestation of the promise, but it surely will come. In the same way I trusted my mother's promise and my children can trust my promise, surely we can trust what God says in His Word about our life and health situations. He never lies. He is the truth.

> *As you pray for things, you have to believe that what you've prayed for has already been granted to you.*

There are three different steps mentioned in Mark 11:24. The first step is to ask in prayer, the second step is to believe, and the third step is to receive. So God wants you to ask Him for things in prayer. But once you pray, He wants you to believe that He will answer your prayers. Then, when you believe He will answer, you will receive what you've asked for. God wants us to pray. Prayer can spark faith in people. In Matthew 18:19 Jesus said, *"Again I say unto you, That if two of you shall agree on earth as touching any thing that they shall ask, it shall be done for them of my Father which is in heaven."* There is a special, communal power when two people pray together.

In James 1:6 it says, *"But let him ask in faith, nothing wavering. For he that wavereth is like a wave of the sea driven with the wind and tossed."* So once you ask, you must have faith, because it's only faith that will cause you to receive what you've asked for. Then, in James 1:7 it says, *"For let not that man think that he shall receive any thing of the Lord."* Doubt will stop your prayers from being answered.

So according to James 1:6–7, asking for something and receiving it are connected together by faith. If you need healing in your body, you have to go to God in prayer and ask Him to touch you. But if after you've prayed you say to yourself, "What if it doesn't work?" then you've just cancelled out everything you've prayed for. God's Word cannot come to pass in your life if you have doubts about it. After you pray for healing, you have to believe that you are going to be healed. Believing, in this case, simply means changing your mind and way of thinking to line up with what the Word of God says. Expect that healing will come exactly as the Word of God says!

We read in 1 Peter 2:24, *"Who his own self bare our sins in his own body on the tree, that we, being dead to sins, should live unto righteousness: by whose stripes ye were healed."* The verb in this sentence was written in past tense, meaning you have already been healed. Healing has already been given to you. Now you have to receive it by faith.

So faith is what takes you from asking to receiving. But what is faith? There is a biblical definition found in Hebrews 11:1: *"Now faith is the substance of things hoped for, the evidence of things not seen."* There may be some things that you hope to receive in your life. Faith is the assurance of those things that you hope for—meaning, because of faith, you are sure that you will receive what you hope to receive even before it happens.

Faith is also the proof of things not seen. Sometimes, after you've prayed for things, you may not see the results right away. Well, faith is the proof or the evidence of things you cannot see—meaning, faith gives you peace that you have received what you've prayed for, even though you cannot see it with your natural eyes yet. In other words, you believe it before you receive the manifestation of what you believe. You are calling things that are not as though they are (Romans 4:17).

Even God calls those things that are not as though they are, according to Romans 4:17. In accordance with this verse, we can see that God is calling Abraham a *"father of many nations"* (Genesis 17:4–5) before he had any children. Abraham's name used to be Abram, but God changed it to Abraham, which meant *"father of many nations."* In other words, God was speaking to Abraham that which He wanted to see manifested in Abraham's life, even though at that time it was only there by faith. When Abraham would be asked, "Sir, what's your name?" he would introduce himself with, "My name is Abraham." In other words, Abraham was saying, "My name is *father of many nations.*" Repeatedly speaking and hearing his name as *"father of many nations,"* even though at that time he was almost a hundred years old, inspired faith in his heart. And sure enough, after three months of confessing God's Word and speaking those things that are not as though they are, he did become a father of many nations.

God did the same thing at creation. He spoke when there was nothing, and everything that we see was created. Our bodies might be sick right now, but change will not come unless we start speaking and believing that healing is coming our way. By speaking and believing, we are prophesying *"those things which be not as though they were"* (Romans 4:17). In Jesus' name and by His stripes we are healed, indeed (Isaiah 53:5b, 1 Peter 2:24b).

Faith is so important if you want God to answer your prayers. According to Mark 11:24, Jesus wants you to ask for things in prayer. But once you ask Him, He wants you to believe what you have asked for. That means having faith, trust, and confidence that He will give you what you've asked for. As you pray for things that are in line with God's Word, and as you believe without wavering, through your faith, those things will come into existence in your life.

Ask and Receive

It says in 1 John 5:14–15, *"And this is the confidence that we have in him, that, if we ask any thing according to his will, he heareth us: And if we know that he hear us, whatsoever we ask, we know that we have the petitions that we desired of him."* Now that we have been born again, we have a special relationship with Jesus. Because of that special relationship, we have the confidence, assurance, and privilege of boldness to come to God. We have free access to God because of what Jesus has accomplished on the cross at Calvary.

It's the same way with children and their parents. Children have free access into their parents' home because they are their children. They have the privilege of eating at their parents' table and enjoying whatever benefits God has bestowed upon their parents, just because they were born into that family. Since we belong to the family of God, we have free access to come to God with boldness.

> *We have to make our requests in accordance with His will, meaning our requests should line up with His plans and purposes for our lives.*

We read in verse 14b, *"If we ask any thing according to his will, he heareth us."* That's an important thing to remember. We have to make our requests in accordance with His will, meaning our requests should line up with His plans and purposes for our lives.

A couple of years ago, I was teaching my children about prayer from the Word of God and my son Joshua asked, "Daddy, does this mean I can ask God for anything and He'll give it to me?"

"Yes," I said.

"I can pray any prayer and God will answer it?" he asked.

"Yes, because that's what He says in His Word. If you ask in line with God's Word, you will receive," I answered.

So he said, "Okay, Lord Jesus, I ask You to send me a cheque for a million dollars in the mailbox tomorrow in Jesus' name. Amen."

The next morning, the first thing Joshua did was run to the mailbox. When he didn't find a cheque for a million dollars, he said to me, "Daddy, it doesn't work. Prayer doesn't work."

I said, "Did you ask God in line with the Word of God? Did God direct you from His Word to pray for a million dollars?"

"No," he answered.

"Did His Spirit speak to your heart and lead you to ask for a million dollars?" I asked.

"No," he answered again.

So I said, "If you didn't ask God in accordance to His will, He will not answer your prayer. You have to pray in line with God's will. When you do, He will answer."

How do we know what God's plans are? Well, we know the will of God by reading the Word of God. God reveals His will to us in His Word. The Word of God is a treasure to be explored. We are to search the Scriptures for God's will. The Word of God is His will. Once we know what His will is for our lives, we are to make our requests known to Him.

There is so much power when we pray in line with God's will. God promises to hear us. If we know He hears us, we can be sure He'll answer our prayers. That's exactly what it says in 1 John 5:15. If we pray in line with His Word, it will be done for us.

When we pray, we can rest assured that Jesus, who hears our prayers, will answer us.

I have six children and they know that when I promise them something, I'm faithful to keep my promises. That's why I don't make too many promises. But let's say I did forget a promise that I made to them. What would they do? They'd remind me of it. How do you think I, as a human father, would feel when my children came to me and said, "Daddy, you promised you would do this for us." How would I feel when they spoke my words back to me?

I'd feel obligated to do whatever I promised them. Actually, I'd be more than willing to do it because I gave them my word that I would. If I, as a human father, am more than willing to fulfill my word to my children, how much more would our heavenly father want to fulfill His Word in our lives?

Jesus promised He would answer our prayers in John 14:13–14: *"And whatsoever ye shall ask in my name, that will I do, that the Father may be glorified in the Son. If ye shall ask any thing in my name, I will do it."* When we pray, we can rest assured that Jesus, who hears our prayers, will answer us. Our requests will be granted to us if we pray in the name of Jesus. The very moment we pray, we know we have received what we've prayed for. Jesus said in Matthew 7:8a, *"For every one that asketh receiveth."* When we ask God for something, we know that, in the spiritual realm, we've already received that which we've asked for.

Now, in regards to the manifestation of what we've asked for, it could happen instantaneously or it might take time. I read about a lady who wore glasses and couldn't see very well without them, so she had to wear them all the time. One day, she heard a message that if we confess with our mouths and declare that we are healed by the stripes of Jesus, we are healed. So she went to her pastor and said, "Pastor, I am healed. I'm going to stomp on my glasses and drive home without them!"

But the pastor said, "I'm glad you are confessing and believing that you are healed. But in order to act based on that confession, you need to experience the manifestation of that healing first. It's like when you plant a seed. You don't receive the fruit right away. It takes time. You need to see the manifestation of the fruit before you can harvest it. So I suggest you don't stomp on your glasses just yet. Keep wearing them until you receive the manifestation."

But this lady didn't listen. She decided to stop wearing her glasses altogether. She drove home without them and continued to live her life with difficulties seeing. Then she started developing headaches. So she came back to her pastor and said, "Pastor, I've been confessing that I'm healed, but now I have headaches."

The pastor said, "I told you to wait until the manifestation happens. So why don't you start wearing your glasses again? But keep on confessing that you are healed by the stripes of Jesus, regardless of the outside circumstances." This time, she listened to her pastor.

The headaches went away, but after awhile, they came back again. So she went to the pastor again and said, "Pastor, when I started wearing my glasses again, my headaches went away. But now that I'm wearing my glasses all the time, my headaches came back."

And the pastor said, "The manifestation of your healing is here. This is the time to stop wearing your glasses, because God has given you the manifestation of healing." She took her glasses off and never had to wear them again.

That's what we need to do. We need to keep on confessing until the manifestation of what we've been confessing happens. If we pray that God will heal us but still feel the symptoms of sickness, it doesn't mean God hasn't healed us. The moment we prayed for healing, we received our healing in the spiritual realm. But in terms of the manifestation in the physical world, we now have to act based on that prayer of faith. Then God will remove the symptoms. (Sometimes it might be required of us to take the steps outlined in Chapter Four, the next chapter of this book, prior to getting the full manifestation of our healing.)

Regardless of what our needs are, we have free access through the blood of Jesus to come before God with boldness. As we line up our requests with His will and according to His Word, we can be sure that we will receive what we've asked for. God wants us to have a relationship of trust, confidence, and faith with Him. He wants us to believe that once we pray for something, we will receive it. If God said it, that settles it. So let us become people who will ask and receive.

As You Have Believed...

In Matthew 8:13 we read, *"And Jesus said unto the centurion, Go thy way; and as thou hast believed, so be it done unto thee. And his servant was healed in the selfsame hour."* This was a word that Jesus Christ spoke to the centurion. In verse 6, we read that when the centurion came to Him, he said, *"Lord, my servant lieth at home sick of the palsy, grievously tormented."* So in verse 7, Jesus said that He would come and restore the boy to health again.

But in verse 8, we read that the centurion replied, *"Lord, I am not worthy that thou shouldest come under my roof: but speak the word only, and my servant shall be healed."* It's amazing how much faith this centurion had. He didn't need Jesus to come and touch his servant boy for him to be healed. He believed that all he needed was for Jesus to speak the word, and healing would come. Jesus was so amazed that, in verse 10c, He said, *"Verily I say unto you, I have not found so great faith, no, not in Israel."*

There is such a great truth to learn from this story. Based on this centurion's faith, trust, and confidence in the words of Jesus, he received what he wanted. Jesus said in verse 13, *"Go thy way; and as thou hast believed, so be it done unto thee. And his servant was healed in the selfsame hour."* So your faith in the Word of God will cause the things that you believe for to become a reality in your life. If you believe that the words of Jesus will come to pass in your life, you will receive whatever you believe.

After Jesus, the greatest friend that you could ever have is yourself. After Satan, the greatest enemy that you could ever have is yourself as well. If you start developing feelings of defeat, you will stay defeated because you will think it, speak it, and act on it. But if you start believing that you will be victorious, victory will come to you, because you will begin to speak whatever your heart believes, and as you speak words of victory and success you will begin to act based on those words. Because of your confession and your action, you will become victorious.

You can achieve anything in life as long as you first believe it in your heart and then confess it with your mouth. Once you do those things, your actions need to line up with your words, and your outcome will be whatever you believed.

If God can cure incurable diseases—if God can raise people from the dead—then He can surely heal you.

Our second youngest daughter, Elisabeth, is a very loveable girl. Before she was born, the doctors discovered that she had an abdominal growth that could cause cystic fibrosis, an incurable disease. The doctors told us that most children with cystic fibrosis die within the first three or four years because they're unable to breathe normally. Mucus builds up in their lungs and they can die from choking on their own mucus. Some children continue to live longer but with great difficulties.

When the doctors said that there was no cure, we understood that there was no medical cure. But we knew there was a supernatural cure. So we asked people to pray that God would heal our baby. Two months later, Ljiljana heard a voice in her spirit saying, "It is done. Do not cry anymore. Do not ask anymore. Just praise Me. It is done."

When we went for another ultrasound at St. Joseph's hospital in Hamilton, Ontario, Dr. Lamont compared the second set of pictures with the first set. And Dr. Lamont said, "I can't find it. The growth isn't there anymore."

Ljiljana shouted, "Praise the Lord!"

I said to Dr. Lamont, "You know, hundreds of people have prayed that God would heal this baby." When he heard the word "prayer," he examined the pictures again. But he still couldn't find the growth.

So he said, "Something must have worked." But that something was some*one*—it was Jesus. Jesus healed our baby! When Elisabeth was born, she was completely healthy, and she has been healthy to this day.

If God can cure incurable diseases—if God can raise people from the dead—then He can surely heal you. He wants you to be healed. But He wants you to mix your faith with words of healing. In Mark 11:22 we read, *"And Jesus answering saith unto them, Have faith in God."* When you have faith in God, according to the next verse, you can speak to the mountain of sickness (or any other mountain in your life) and command it to leave your body in Jesus' name. And that mountain of sickness *has* to obey.

That's exactly what it says in Mark 11:24: *"Therefore I say unto you, What things soever ye desire, when ye pray, believe that ye receive them, and ye shall have them."* "What things soever ye desire" certainly includes the desire for complete healing.

Jesus promises that it will be done for you as you have believed. But your outcome in life cannot exceed your level of faith. You will always achieve what you believe. If you believe that you'll just barely get by in life, that's all you'll achieve. But if you believe you can achieve greater things, you will achieve greater things in your life. You have a tremendous influence on your circumstances.

As I said, after Jesus, your greatest friend is yourself, because your thoughts, words, and actions will determine your future. So believe the Word of God, trust the words of Jesus, and have faith! Those words will come to pass in your life.

We can see that there is a great deal we have to do in order to receive God's supernatural healing in our lives. We know from the Scriptures that God healed in the Old Testament. He healed in the New Testament, and He heals today. But whether or not we receive healing depends on what we do with the word of healing that God gives us. We need to take the word of healing, believe it, confess it, stand upon it, and act based on that word until we receive the manifestation of our healing.

But sometimes that may not be enough. As I mentioned earlier, we have to do our part to receive healing. Our part does consist of praying, confessing, and believing. But more often than not there are other things we need to do as well. In the Old Testament, we read a story about the Israelites at the entrance of the Promised Land. God said to them, *"Behold, I have set the land before you: go in and possess the land which the LORD sware unto your fathers, Abraham, Isaac, and Jacob, to give unto them and to their seed after them"* (Deuteronomy 1:8). We can see clearly that God is *giving* them the land, but we can also see clearly that for the Israelites to get the land that God is giving them they have to *go in* and *possess* the land. In other words, there is something the Israelites have to do—in this case, fight for the land—if they are to take what God is giving them.

This is true in every aspect of our lives. If we are to take what God is giving us, we need to do something for it. It might be that all we need to do is accept, believe, and trust the Word of God that we are healed in Christ Jesus. But it might be that we must do something else, like fighting for what the Lord promised to give us. It really varies from one situation to another. God heals us supernaturally, but there are things we can do to help our bodies heal naturally.

Now that we've discussed the soul aspect of healing, let's move on to the body aspect and talk about ways of achieving natural healing through a change of lifestyle.

In Chapter Four, I share some insightful information about different biblically based ways to promote natural healing, and I outline some excellent strategies for keeping your body healthy. If you've become sick because of lack of knowledge about what constitutes a healthy lifestyle, you'll find the following chapter especially helpful. Let us proceed to the next chapter together and discuss more about the body and how you can achieve natural healing through your actions.

CHAPTER FOUR
Body: Natural Healing

*"And by the river upon the bank thereof, on this side
and on that side, shall grow all trees for meat, whose
leaf shall not fade, neither shall the fruit thereof be
consumed: it shall bring forth new fruit according to
his months, because their waters they issued out of
the sanctuary: and the fruit thereof shall be for meat,
and the leaf thereof for medicine"* (Ezekiel 47:12).

We can see here that God has created food for us by creating fruits, vegetables, and water. The fruit is for meat (meaning food), and the leaves are for medicine. There are many large animals that don't eat meat. They eat vegetables. God intended for us to eat fruits and vegetables and various seeds. There are powerful elements of healing in the very things that God created for us in nature.

In Exodus 23:25 we read, *"And ye shall serve the LORD your God, and he shall bless thy bread, and thy water; and I will take sickness away from the*

God intended for us to eat fruits and vegetables more than meat.

midst of thee." It says here that we are to serve the Lord our God. In other words, we are to engage in things that are pleasing to God. When we serve the Lord, He will bless our bread, which is our food. Not only that, but He'll bless our water. Then He'll take away our sicknesses.

The blessing of food and water comes prior to sicknesses being removed from our midst. So we can see from this passage that serving God is the prerequisite for receiving the blessing of God upon our food and

Our food and water are supposed to be our medicine.

water. Then our food and water, which has been blessed by God, becomes the source of our healing. Our food and water are supposed to be our medicine. That's how God takes sicknesses away from our midst. Even Hippocrates, the father of modern medicine, said, "Our food should be our medicine. Our medicine should be our food."[7]

Obesity is a huge problem in North America, especially childhood obesity.[8] Over sixty percent of North Americans are obese; in Canada fifty-nine percent of adults are overweight or obese, and in the United States seventy-one percent of adults are overweight or obese.[9] All kinds of sicknesses—like diabetes, some cancers, heart attacks, strokes, allergies, and arthritic pain—come as a result of obesity. "Obesity is two times more deadly than cigarettes, alcoholism, and drunk driving put together."[10] If we don't receive God's blessing upon our food and water, and if we don't have the proper balance and proportions of food and water, we can't expect to be healthy.

If you, as a believer, have gone to the altar to receive prayer for healing, that's great! If you've called a ministry and asked someone to pray for you to get healed, that's wonderful! God wants us to pray for each other. But you've also got to be willing to do something for your healing to come, because God will not do your part for you. You've got to take active measures to improve your health. For example, God will not run around the block so that you can get in shape, as I was hoping He would do for me at one time. *After all, it is easier for Him to run around the block,* I thought.

God will not run around the block so that you can get in shape.

In Deuteronomy 8:18a we read, *"But thou shalt remember the LORD thy God: for it is he that giveth thee power to get wealth."* God gives you the power to create wealth, but He doesn't give you the wealth. You are the one who has to exercise that power of God to create wealth for yourself. In this case, God is the one who blesses your food and water, but you've got to be obedient to Him and you've got to eat and drink the proper foods if you want to be healed. God will not do it for you. You can't expect God to heal you if you're purposely putting unhealthy food and unclean water into your body. That food is not blessed of God.

In Deuteronomy 30:9a we read, *"And the LORD thy God will make thee plenteous in every work of thine hand."* Many people have the misconception that they can succeed at something without working at it. But the only time success comes before work is in the dictionary. In real life, you have to work if you want to receive success, because it is the *"work of thine hand"* that God blesses. That means if you don't put your hands to work (by doing your part to get healthy, for example), God cannot bless you with good health.

It says in Deuteronomy 28:8a, *"The LORD shall command the blessing upon thee in thy storehouses, and in all that thou settest thine hand unto."* Notice that God will bless everything that *"thou settest thine hand unto."* In

"In all labor there is profit, but idle chatter leads only to poverty." —Proverbs 14:23, NKJV

other words, you have to do something before God can bless you. You have to work! You have to make some changes in your lifestyle in order for God to heal you. There is no way you can be successful in life without labour.

Many of us have heard of healing ministries. Some of them are good and some are not. The issue of who is good and who is not goes beyond the questions of this book. I have a different point to make. They often preach about healing and many people get healed at various crusades.

But on some occasions, some people get sick again soon after getting healed. One such ministry hired Dr. Don Colbert, a Christian medical doctor, to find out why this was happening.

"Go to the ant, thou sluggard; consider her ways, and be wise: Which having no guide, overseer, or ruler, provideth her meat in the summer, and gathereth her food in the harvest."
—Proverbs 6:6-8

Dr. Colbert followed up with many of the people who were healed at various healing services to find out where they were going after the crusades. He saw that they were going to McDonald's, doughnut shops, and other fast food restaurants. They were eating all the same foods that got them sick in the first place. That's why a lot of their sicknesses came back.

God wants us to ask Him for healing and then do our part to receive and keep our healing. If I save money, will you have more in your pocket? If you run around the block, will I burn the calories? No. So the same applies to our healing. God wants us to do our part for our healing to come. God will not do our part for us. God will not exercise or eat properly for us. We have to do what we need to do. We have to serve God and obey His Word regarding our health. When we serve Him, He blesses our food and water and takes sicknesses away from us (Exodus 23:25).

The Purpose of Medication

"For by thy sorceries were all nations deceived" (Revelation 18:23c).

The word "sorceries" comes from the Greek word *phar-ma-kia*, which in the English language is translated as drugs. According to Webster's Dictionary, a drug is defined as a substance other than food intended to affect the structure or function of the body. God never made our bodies to intake foreign substances like drugs, whether they are legal or illegal.

NATURAL HEALING

There are many people who ignore the natural elements of healing that God gave us (which we will discuss in more detail in this chapter) and go straight to drugs and medications, hoping to get healed that way.

The real purpose of drugs is to control the symptoms of a sickness, not to cure the sickness itself.

Usually people who are sick go to the doctor, get a prescription, go to the pharmacy, pick up their medication, and then go home and take the drugs, thinking every pill in that bottle is a miracle pill that'll magically make their sicknesses go away. It's interesting to note that some doctors may prescribe certain medications because of the persuasion of some pharmaceutical salespeople, and that might not always be in the best interest of the patient.[11]

But have you ever wondered what drugs really do? The real purpose of drugs is to control the symptoms of a sickness, not to cure the sickness itself. But very often while they're doing that, they're also hurting some good parts of our bodies that aren't sick at all. Similar things can be said about surgeries and other standard medical approaches.

My mother-in-law lives in Vienna, Austria, and just recently she had to go through a time in the hospital. She's not a believer. She had to go to the hospital because her blood pressure wasn't doing well. The doctors concluded that the reason for her heart troubles was the multiple medications she was taking. The medications were working against each other, which almost caused her to die at a very young age of sixty-two years.

My father, who was seventy-eight years old, went to the hospital in Belgrade, Serbia for some leg pain and they admitted him into the hospital. However, through some misdiagnosis, he was offered a strong medication that caused him to have a massive stroke, which led to death shortly thereafter. He could have lived a few more years, but his life was shortened through the wrong medication prescribed to him.

Hospital deaths due to medical errors in the United States, as estimated by both the Institute of Medicine (IOM) and the Journal of the

American Medical Association (JAMA), are in the top ten causes of death, with ratings from position 5 (JAMA) to position 9 (IOM). These reports are based only on hospital admissions. The real number of deaths from medical errors in a doctor's office, such as misdiagnosis or delayed treatment, is most likely higher.[12]

Besides the Word of God within our hearts, our immune system is another major secret God uses to cure our bodies.

Whenever we experience symptoms of sickness, we need to understand that those symptoms are not an invitation for medication. God installed warning signals in our bodies to remind us that it's time to cleanse our bodies of accumulated toxic waste. For example, headaches, a runny nose, or any other symptoms are signals that it's time for a cleansing. Drugs are poisonous toxins. There is no way we can be drugged or poisoned into health. More often than not, drugs create problems rather than solve them. What we need to do is cleanse our bodies from toxins and allow our bodies to heal themselves.

The human body has been created in such a way that it heals itself. It heals itself through the body's immune system. Besides the Word of God within our hearts, our immune system is another major secret God uses to cure our bodies. Hippocrates said, "Everyone has a doctor in him or her; we just have to help it in its work. The natural healing force within each one of us is the greatest force in getting well."[13] The healing is really primarily internal and is not external.

For example, if you were to cut yourself and you never did anything for it, that wound would eventually heal by itself. A scab would develop over the wound, and in time that scab would fall off and there would be new skin under-underneath. Sometimes if

Everyone has a doctor in him or her; we just have to help it in its work. The natural healing force within each one of us is the greatest force in getting well.
— Hippocrates

there's a lot of bleeding, you would need to apply some kind of medication on the cut to protect the wound from becoming infected. But that medication only protects the wound; it doesn't influence the healing process.

The human body's immune system is created to heal the body, and the stronger we make our immune systems, the more capable they will be in fighting off sickness. Our immune systems are complex networks of cells, tissues, and organs working around the clock to keep us healthy. Our immune systems make tiny proteins called antibodies which fight off foreign invaders by recognizing, eliminating, or neutralizing against millions of bacteria, microbes, fungi, viruses, infections, toxins, and other organisms that can invade the body. That's why it's so important that we have a strong immune system. If we have a weak immune system, it'll be easier for us to catch sickness.

Did you know that up to 80% percent of our body's immune system cells are found in the digestive tract (stomach, small intestine, and large intestine)? Proper nutrition helps our digestive tract to stay healthy, keeping our immune systems and bodies healthy. It is obvious that our immune system and digestive tract work together to keep us healthy.

You may ask, "What are some things we do that weaken our immune system?" We weaken our immune system by not eating properly, not drinking enough water or only drinking tap water or soda pops, not getting enough rest, living under stress, not exercising on a regular basis, and not cleansing our bodies of poisonous toxins. Those are all ways of weakening our immune system, making it easier for us to get sick.

Now what are some ways we can strengthen our immune system? The things that strengthen our immune system are the opposite of those that weaken it. For example, we can avoid or properly prepare ahead of time for stress in our lives, drink enough water, eat the right foods, get enough rest, exercise regularly, cleanse and detoxify our bodies on a frequent basis, and take some daily supplements. Those are some of the things we can do to strengthen our immune system. Let us discuss each of them in more detail.

Reducing Stress

"A merry heart doeth good like a medicine" (Proverbs 17:22a).

There are many toxic emotions that can negatively affect our health, such as guilt, bitterness, resentment, and stress. Those feelings are some of the most destructive emotions we can have. You can be doing everything else right, like eating properly and exercising regularly, but if you have those toxic emotions in your heart, those emotions can have a tremendously negative effect on your health.

The solution for getting rid of guilt is, as I said, to obtain the forgiveness of God. We know through the Word of God that Jesus Christ has died on the cross at Calvary and paid the penalty for our sins. Because of what Jesus has done, there is no way God can punish you for your sins if you confess your sins to Him. Seeking the forgiveness of God is so important for removing any feelings of guilt you may have.

A solution for getting rid of feelings of bitterness and resentment could be granting forgiveness to someone else. You may be bitter toward your mother, father, brother, sister, friend, or enemy. But being bitter toward anybody is only going to hurt you. Those feelings of resentment destroy your immune system's ability to fight off sicknesses, making it easier for you to become sick. Not to mention, it is also poisoning your relationships with other people.

In Matthew 6:14–15 Jesus said, *"For if ye forgive men their trespasses, your heavenly Father will also forgive you: But if ye forgive not men their trespasses, neither will your Father forgive your trespasses."* In Romans 12:18 we read, *"If it be possible, as much as lieth in you, live peaceably with all men."* That's what God wants you to do in order to be healthy. You have to free yourself from any feelings of bitterness or resentment by forgiving those who have wronged you. Let me remind you here of the study done by Dr. Michael Linden's team in Berlin (mentioned in the previous chapter), which has shown that various serious diseases can be caused by a prolonged state of bitterness.

So it's important to accept the forgiveness of God, and then through that to be enabled to grant forgiveness to others in Jesus' name. It doesn't mean you have to agree with what that oth-

> *It's important to accept the forgiveness of God, and then through that to be enabled to grant forgiveness to others in Jesus' name.*

er person has said or done to you. It just means you have to release yourself from the bondage of feeling resentful toward that person.

Now, in regards to getting rid of stress, the solution is laughter, as we read in Proverbs 17:22a: *"A merry heart doeth good like a medicine."* You can laugh yourself to health because laughter is good medicine.

When we are sick, the first tendency we have is to go to the Lord in prayer. Secondly, we have the tendency to go and see a doctor. Usually the doctor will prescribe some medication to us. If we take that medication, it's supposed to attack the virus or infection in our bodies and stop it from spreading or becoming worse. Then our bodies are supposed to recover to complete health through the work of our own immune system. But aside from physical medication, Proverbs 17:22a teaches us that there is a greater form of medication that will strengthen our health. Actually, even medical researchers are discovering the benefits of this type of medication.

According to that verse, a merry heart is good like medicine. The heart of a person represents his or her thoughts, feelings, and emotions. So really, the heart represents the person. So a merry person is good medicine! There is a German saying that goes, *"Wer lacht lebt länger."* In English, this translates to, *"He who laughs lives longer."* Doctors have discovered that ten minutes of laughter a day is tremendously good for our health.[14] When we have a belly laugh, meaning we laugh out of our hearts and we're not just forcing laughter out, we relieve a lot of stress that we've accumulated throughout the day. That time of laughter will have a healing effect on our bodies. So watch some funny videos and have an enjoyable time together with your family.

We also need to do what we can to avoid as much stress as possible. For that purpose, we need to identify the stress points in our lives. Stress is caused by our inner response to the influence of either external or internal stressors. At the moment of stress, there is an outpouring of adrenaline (a stimulant hormone) into the bloodstream.

Some external stressors are:

1) Environmental: noise, bright lights, heat, crowded spaces.
2) Social: rudeness, bossiness, or aggressiveness from others.
3) Structural: rules, regulations, deadlines.
4) Significant life events: death of a loved one, loss of a job, promotion, a new baby.
5) Incidental: slow traffic, lost keys, car breakdown.

Some internal stressors are:

1) Lifestyle choices: caffeine, lack of sleep, too much work, debt and mortgage.
2) Negative attitude: pessimism, criticism.
3) Mental: unrealistic expectations, taking things too personally, now-or-never thinking, exaggerating.
4) Personality type: tends towards perfectionism, works too much, wants to please everybody, inflexibility.

We should prepare ahead of time for these stressors as best we can. That way we will diminish the effects or eliminate some of the stress points altogether. We should make sure we add fun to our days by enjoying our spouse, our children, and ourselves. Also, we can read a funny book, tell and listen to wholesome jokes or funny stories, watch some funny home videos

He who laughs lives longer.
– German saying

with our families, and have an enjoyable experience in nature. All of those things will create a merry heart, and having a merry heart is a great way to get rid of stress.

Drinking Plenty of Water

"You must serve only the LORD your God. If you do, I will bless you with food and water, and I will keep you healthy" (Exodus 23:25, NLT).

As I said, our food and water are the sources for keeping us healthy. I'll discuss more about food later, but for now I want to talk about the importance of drinking enough water. From a physical point of view, water is the most important element for our bodies. We can only survive about four days without water. Eventually our bodies get dehydrated and we die. Water gives us life.

That's why clean and pure water is so important. But in our society, we throw a lot of poisonous chemicals into our water, which pollutes it. Most families have a water purifier, either in their fridge or by their sink. Tap water needs to be purified from all the harsh chemicals in order to be safe for us to drink.

In Ezekiel 47:8–9 we read, *"Then said he unto me, These waters issue out toward the east country, and go down into the desert, and go into the sea: which being brought forth into the sea, the waters shall be healed. And it shall come to pass, that every thing that liveth, which moveth, whithersoever the rivers shall come, shall live: and there shall be a very great multitude of fish, because these waters shall come thither: for they shall be healed; and every thing shall live whither the river cometh."* God has brought healing and life through water. In Revelation 22:1 we read, *"And he shewed me a pure river of water of life, clear as crystal, proceeding out of the throne of God and of the Lamb."* Again, water is a source of life.

Did you know that your body is about seventy percent water? Did you know this planet's surface is about seventy percent water as well? And seeing as both people and the earth come from the same Creator, that explains the design. Since we are more water than anything else, we need water more than we need solid food. Muscles are about seventy-five percent water; brain cells are about eighty-five percent water; blood is about eighty-two percent water; and bones are approximately twenty-five percent water.[15] So since your body is mostly made of water, it's important to keep your body hydrated with clean water.

Since your body is mostly made of water, it's important to keep your body hydrated with clean water.

If you don't drink enough water, your body won't have the opportunity to cleanse itself. So the water inside you becomes stale, which can cause sicknesses. Think of a puddle of water on the ground that never changes. Eventually that puddle becomes stale and starts to stink. The same thing happens in our bodies. We need to keep replenishing the water inside our bodies by drinking clean water and flushing the old water out.

Water is one of the most important nutrients we need to give our bodies. It is a miracle cure, indeed. But we shouldn't count caffeinated and sugared beverages into that because caffeine and sugar steal water from our bodies. They're doing more harm than good. That's often why we have many physical ailments. Water is a miracle medicine that God created for us to enjoy every day of our lives. If people have ailments, they should start drinking more pure water.

According to Dr. Don Colbert, headaches, back pain, arthritis, joint pain, skin problems, dry skin, allergies, heart burn, constipation, memory loss, digestion problems, and many other health problems are often caused by dehydration. People with those ailments have come to him for help and he has often prescribed water. In two weeks, they didn't have those problems any longer.[16]

Water is the main lubricant for our joints. Many people suffer from arthritis and it could be because they don't drink enough water. There is no need for us to have back pain. Those joints need lubrication from water. So when we drink enough water, we help prevent rubbing of the bones in our backs. The best medicine for arthritic pain is water.

In addition, water increases our immune system efficiency and prevents clogging of the arteries in our heart and brain. It helps to reduce the risk of heart attack and stroke. Water is connected to brain functions. It is needed to manufacture serotonin (a feel-good chemical and key neurotransmitter necessary for communication between nerve cells), melatonin (a sleep hormone and powerful antioxidant, anti-aging, and anti-depressant produced by our own brain), and various other hormones made by the brain. Water helps to prevent memory loss. It reduces the risk of Alzheimer's, sclerosis, and Parkinson's disease.

Water even affects our appearance and removes the affects of aging. It makes our skin smoother and gives it a sparkling lustre. The more water we drink, the better our face is going to look. The less water we drink, the more wrinkles we're going to have. Water is the best beautifying agent, so ladies, take notice.

Alkaline water is the best water you can drink... Our bodies thrive on alkaline water because it helps us detoxify our bodies.

When you don't have enough water in your body, your system dehydrates. When that happens, you build up acidity in your body. Acidity is the primary cause of most sicknesses. As already mentioned, according to Dr. Don Colbert, headaches, back pain, arthritis, joint pain, skin problems, dry skin, allergies, heartburn, constipation, memory loss, digestion, and many other health problems are all caused by lack of water and dehydration.[17]

How much water should we drink? If we take our weight in pounds and divide that number in half, we'll see how many ounces of water we need to drink per day. Let's say you're 160 pounds. That means you need about eighty ounces of water each day. Eight ounces is one cup, so you need about ten cups of water every single day. Most of us need about two to three litres of water on a daily basis (don't forget to count into this the water contained within fruits and vegetables which on a daily basis amounts to about one litre). One of the best strategies for keeping healthy is to drink plenty of fresh water daily. We shouldn't wait to be thirsty to do so. If we feel thirsty, we're already too late.

When's the best time to drink water? We should drink water throughout the day, regardless of whether or not we feel thirsty. But it's important to remember that we should drink at least one to two cups of water thirty minutes before our meals and two hours after our meals. Before a main meal, we should drink two to three cups of water to avoid overeating. And while we eat, we shouldn't drink more than one cup of water, otherwise we will flush out a lot of good enzymes and nutrients from our food prior to them being absorbed into our system. Also, we shouldn't drink after 7:00 p.m., so we can sleep better.

Keep in mind that I'm not talking about drinking just any kind of water. Many health experts believe that our low-quality tap water can pose health concerns, so some people have resorted to bottled water, thinking that's the safest water they can drink. But some bottled water is actually just reprocessed tap water from cities around the country. In fact, one-fourth of bottled water is really just tap water.[18]

Alkaline water is the best water you can drink. Since the majority of the foods we eat create acid wastes in our system, it is important to drink alkaline water in order to maintain optimal health and energy, particularly because acid water is a hotbed of microorganisms, bacteria, and viruses.

Acid wastes (not only from food and drink but also from stress and other pollutants) are dumped into the bloodstream and lymph. Then they are transported to the liver and kidneys for the detoxification process. The pH level of our internal fluids affects every living cell in our bodies, and the effect that over-acidification can have upon the health of our bodies is immense.

If we just drink enough water, we'll sleep better, feel better, our joints will ache a lot less, and we could avoid many diseases.

Alkaline water helps neutralize acids and remove toxins from the body. So, our bodies thrive on alkaline water because it helps us detoxify our bodies. It also acts as a conductor of electrochemical activity from cell to cell. Ideally, water should have a pH value of nine or ten. As we keep our bodies properly hydrated, we'll develop more of a thirst for water. It's important to understand that food cravings are often the body's cry for water.

So how do we ensure that we're feeding our bodies with the right kind of water? It's important to make sure our water is filtered. You can do that by using a handy, affordable filter such as a Brita. However, if you're looking for full, life-giving, energy-boosting nourishment from your water, try the following techniques.

Get a home water distiller, which heats tap water electrically to the boiling point. The purified condensation then drains into a clean container, leaving all the impurities behind in the boiling chamber. This process kills and removes bacteria, viruses, cysts, and heavy metals. Distilled water transports inorganic minerals and toxins out of the body, helping to cleanse and purify the body's internal environment. Since distilled water has more oxygen ions and fewer hydrogen ions, the water is far less acidic and more alkaline than other types of water.

You can also get a water ionizer. By using a water ionizer, you will be running the water over positive and negative electrodes. This process separates the water into alkaline (seventy percent) and acidic (thirty percent). Then the alkaline water is used for drinking, while the acidic water can be used on the outside of the body since it is proven to kill many types of bacteria. Ionized water is the only type of water that has a low surface tension, which allows for greater absorption of water and nutrients into the body.

Another filter you can get is a reverse osmosis water filter, which utilizes a fine membrane to filter water, a process known as hyperfiltration. This removes bacteria, salts, sugars, proteins, particles, dyes, and other damaging elements. The membrane that is used is semipermeable, which allows the water to pass through while removing the contaminants.

Using a home water distiller, ionizer, or purifier will give you clean water with varying degrees of alkalinity. And it doesn't have to be expensive. You can increase the alkalinity of your drinking water even more by squeezing fresh lemon or lime juice into the water or by adding an alkalizing pH-boosting supplement to the water.

Also, your water source can be found in alkaline foods like fresh fruits and vegetables. Bananas are about seventy percent water, apples are eighty percent water, tomatoes and watermelons are more than ninety percent water, and lettuce is ninety-five percent water. If you eat those healthy fresh fruits and vegetables, they can help you meet your daily water requirement. Ideally, we should be getting about one litre of our daily water intake needs through the foods we eat!

When you and I make sure we drink enough clean water, we are giving our bodies the best nutrients possible. If we just drink enough water, we'll sleep better, feel better, our joints will ache a lot less, and we could avoid many diseases that I mentioned above. As we read in Exodus 23:25, health will come to our bodies because God will bless our food and our water.

Eat Living Food, Not Dead Food

"And out of the ground made the LORD God to grow every trees that is pleasant to the sight, and good for food" (Genesis 2:9a).

God created our food. The best food to eat is the food that God Himself created for us. We read in Genesis 1:29, *"And God said, Behold, I have given you every herb bearing seed, which is upon the face of all the earth, and every tree, in the which is the fruit of a tree yielding seed; to you it shall be for meat."* When we eat the food that God created the way He created it, we're going to be healthy.

The health industry today has concluded that for a person to be healthy, he or she has to eat healthy foods in proper proportions. But what the nutrition industry is teaching today, the

When we eat the food that God created the way He created it, we're going to be healthy.

Bible has taught us from the beginning. A nutritionist will tell us that it's not healthy to eat processed foods, fried foods, or even red meat. When food has been processed or fried, the nourishment is no longer useful to our bodies. So we become hungry again quickly and we eat more. As a result, we gain weight and that's how we become unhealthy and sick.

That's why dieticians will tell us to eat lots of fresh fruits and vegetables, which are alkaline foods when consumed in their organic, natural form. But in the Bible, God has instructed us to do this anyway. In Genesis 2:16 we read, *"And the LORD God commanded the man, saying, Of every tree of the garden thou mayest freely eat."* The major food sources that God gave to us humans before the flood were seeds, fruits, and vegetables. There was no meat consumed at that time. After the flood, God allowed certain meats. But the meat that is sold in today's market is very toxic and not useful for human consumption. It's so important to remember that the healthiest foods we can eat are raw seeds, fresh fruits, and vegetables.

We also read in Ezekiel 47:12c, *"The fruit thereof shall be for meat, and the leaf thereof for medicine."* A similar passage is found in Revelation 22:2: *"In the midst of the street of it, and on either side of the river, was there the tree of life, which bare twelve manner of fruits, and yielded her fruit every month: and the leaves of the tree were for the healing of the nations."* We can see from these passages that the fruit is for our food and the leaves are for our healing.

Keep in mind what Hippocrates said: "Our food should be our medicine. Our medicine should be our food."[19] In other words, God has provided medicine through the food that He's created. When we eat food that He's made—like fruits, vegetables, and seeds in their raw state—the way He created them, we are feeding our bodies with the healthiest forms of medicine possible.

> *Our food should be our medicine. Our medicine should be our food.*

Some sources of alkaline food include fruits like lemons, limes, avocados, tomatoes, grapefruit, watermelon, and rhubarb. Vegetables that are considered alkaline foods are asparagus, artichokes, cabbage, lettuce, onions, cauliflower, radishes, turnips, lamb's lettuce, peas, zucchini, red cabbage, leeks, watercress, spinach, turnip, chives, carrots, green beans, beetroot, garlic, celery, grasses (wheat, straw, and barley), cucumber, broccoli, kale, and Brussels sprouts.

Fruits should be eaten in the morning because they cleanse the toxins within our bodies, and vegetables should be eaten afterwards because they act as builders of our bodies. We should be eating more vegetables than fruits because of the high sugar content in fruit. The darker and greener the vegetables are, and the riper and stronger coloured the fruits are, the better they are for our health. For example, red apples are one of the best fruits we can eat to fight cancer. The apple skins have most of the antioxidants, which help combat cancer. Also, as I mentioned, there are other fruits and vegetables that are healthy for our bodies as well.

But in our western diet, many of us have departed from the way God intended for us to eat. Many of us eat other things more than we eat fresh fruits and vegetables. Or many of us cook our vegetables so much and at such high temperatures (115 degrees Celsius or more) that we actually destroy all the healthy enzymes and over eighty percent of the vitamins. The heat changes even the protein of the food into a state that cannot be used and processed in our bodies. Even the organic minerals become inorganic. So when it comes time to eat the vegetable, we're actually eating it dead. All the nutrients are gone. It's better to eat vegetables in their raw state.

When we eat food that He's made—like fruits, vegetables, and seeds in their raw state—the way He created them, we are feeding our bodies with the healthiest forms of medicine possible.

The same is true with seeds. Sunflower seeds, pumpkin seeds, almonds, and other types of seeds are much better to eat while they're in their raw state. It's better not to cook them, bake them, or salt them. When we eat them in their natural state (in a balanced way), they provide some of the best nutrients to our bodies.

People in Mediterranean climates usually don't eat as much red meat as people here in Western culture do. Instead, they eat more fish, vegetables, olives, and other natural foods. Because of that, they are much healthier. There are fewer heart attacks and other health problems amongst those people. But when they come here and adapt to the diet of Westerners, they start getting similar sicknesses as people here do.

We read in Ezekiel 47:12c that not only should fruit be for food, but also *"the leaf thereof for medicine."* In the Amplified Bible, this part of verse 12 says: *"their leaves for healing"* (AMP). So if there are sicknesses in our bodies, this verse says that the leaves are for healing. Many studies have been conducted to show that there are nutrients within specific leaves that have a healing effect on our bodies.

For example, there are some tea leaves which help us with regularity and overall balanced health. There are other herbs that are healthy as well and have a healing effect on our bodies. Even the medical community has used herbs for creating medicines (e.g. morphine).[20] Those healthy nutrients attack the viruses within our bodies that cause us to be sick. When those viruses stop growing, our bodies have the opportunity to recover on their own. That's why God says here that the leaves are for healing.

The rapidly growing cases of cancer, cardiovascular disease, and diabetes are largely due to the rise in consumption of acid-forming foods such as sugars, saturated fats (like margarine), and white breads. Saturated fat—particularly the kind found in margarine, Crisco, and refined oils—became very popular in the United States before 1920. About ten years after, major heart diseases started to appear.[21] These foods are the major cause of clogged arteries, heart

Living cells in our bodies cannot be nourished with dead food. Death begets death; life begets life. We cannot produce life out of death.

attacks, and strokes. Some other examples of acid-forming foods include meats such as pork, lamb, beef, chicken, turkey, crustaceans, and other seafood (apart from occasional oily fish such as salmon). Other acid-forming foods are milk, eggs, cheese, cream, yogurt, ice cream, fizzy drinks, coffee, tea, white pasta, white bread, sweets, chocolate, microwave meals, powdered soups, and fast food. We should all aim to eat about seventy to eighty percent alkaline foods and a maximum of twenty to thirty percent acid-forming foods.

What are some of the negative effects of eating dead food? Dead food often causes problems with arthritis in the knees, hips, and other joints, in addition to causing headaches, cancer, heart attacks, asthma, and diabetes.

It's not healthy to eat the fat of any animal. The fat and skin of any animal is the worst part of the animal. The fat contains all the poisons and toxins of that animal, so it should never be consumed. That's why God said that the fat should be consumed on the altar because it belongs to Him (Leviticus 3:16). Not only does dead food lead to all kinds of sicknesses, but it could also lead to weight problems. Dead food contains a lot of toxins. Those toxins produce poisons in our bodies, which come in the form of fat. That's why we gain weight when we eat dead food.

In Proverbs 23:20–21 we read, *"Be not among winebibbers; among riotous eaters of flesh: For the drunkard and the glutton shall come to poverty: and drowsiness shall clothe a man with rags."* According to this verse, we shouldn't join those who are drinking and gorging themselves. When you eat food, you may have noticed that an hour later you feel tired and sleepy. That's an indication that you've eaten too much and that you've eaten improper foods. When you eat properly, such as fresh

When you eat food, you may have noticed that an hour later you feel tired and sleepy. That's an indication to you that you've eaten too much and that you've eaten improper foods.

fruits and vegetables and whole grains, you're not going to feel tired after eating.

It's important to remember that living food is anything that is made by God and in as close a state as possible to how God made it. Anything that is manmade has been processed or fried, ruining the state in which God created it. That food is dead. Living cells in our bodies cannot be nourished with dead food. Death begets death; life begets life. We cannot produce life out of death.

Everything you and I put in our mouths has the potential to bring life or death to us. When you and I eat the wrong foods, we're bringing death upon our bodies. But when we eat living food, the good food that God created, and we eat those foods in the state that God created them (raw or close to raw), we are bringing life and health to our bodies. That's the diet that God intended for us to have.

Getting Enough Rest

"The LORD your God hath given you rest" (Joshua 1:13b).

According to Genesis 1, God made the heavens and the earth and everything in them in six days. Then He rested on the seventh. He called the seventh day the Sabbath day. We're supposed to work six days a week and rest every seventh day. We cannot continuously work day after day for more than six days and expect to be healthy. Our bodies will get tired, our immune systems will weaken, we will acquire more stress, and as a result, we could get sick.

During World War II, when the Nazi planes were attacking Britain, some of the British people thought it would be better to work seven days a week as opposed to just six so that they could produce more weapons. Soon afterwards, they realized that they were producing *fewer* weapons when they worked seven days because the workers were tired and less productive. They needed that day of rest in order to work productively. That's why it's so important to take a day of rest every six days.

The Sabbath day is a holy day dedicated unto the Lord. It's a day when we're supposed to cease from all of our work and commit ourselves to God and our families. In addition to the Sabbath day, we read in the Bible that there were other times of rest, such as special festivals and holy days. Three of them were long-term festivals—for example, before the harvest, after the harvest, and during the Passover. Those celebrations consisted of a whole week of festivities, so during that time everybody ceased from their labour and came before the Lord.

In addition to the Sabbath day and those festivities, we also need daily rest. In Joshua 1:13b we read, *"The LORD your God hath given you rest."* It's so important that we get enough rest on a daily basis. One third of our day should be dedicated to resting our bodies. We should sleep at least eight hours a day in order to rest our bodies. Every hour before midnight counts as two hours after midnight.

Sleep architecture follows a pattern of alternating REM (rapid eye movement) and NREM (non-rapid eye movement) sleep throughout a typical night in a cycle that repeats itself about every ninety minutes. NREM, which consumes seventy-five percent of the night's sleep, starts as we begin to fall asleep. NREM sleep involves four stages. Stage one is a light sleep; stage two is an onset of sleep; and stages three and four are the deepest, most restorative periods of sleep. REM sleep takes up twenty-five percent of the night's sleep. This is where dreams occur. REM first occurs about ninety minutes after falling asleep and recurs about every ninety minutes throughout the night, getting longer as the night progresses.[22]

Sleep deprivation has been linked to health problems such as obesity and high blood pressure. Insufficient sleep affects growth hormone secretion that is linked to obesity; as the amount of hormone secretion decreases, the chances of weight gain increases. But when we get enough sleep, we improve our immune system and balance our appetites by helping to regulate levels of the hormones ghrelin and leptin, which play a role in our feelings of hunger and fullness. But when we're sleep deprived, we may feel the need to eat more, which can lead to weight gain.[23]

Also, proper sleep allows blood pressure to fall, but interrupted sleep can adversely affect this normal decline, leading to hypertension and cardiovascular problems. Insufficient sleep impairs the body's ability to use insulin, which can lead to the onset of diabetes. Sleep deprivation also causes negative mood and behaviour, decreased productivity, and safety issues in the home, on the job, and on the road.[24]

Sufficient sleep is important for both your mental and physical health.

When we get sufficient sleep (experts generally recommend an average of seven to nine hours per night), we wake up feeling refreshed and alert for our daily activities. Getting enough rest affects how we look, feel, and perform on a daily basis. It also plays a major role in our overall quality of life.[25]

Some ways to improve your sleep include maintaining a regular bedtime and wakeup time (even on weekends), establishing a relaxing bedtime routine such as soaking in a hot bath and then reading a book or listening to soothing music, not eating at least two to three hours before your regular bedtime, exercising regularly but at least a few hours before bedtime, avoiding caffeine such as coffee, tea, soft drinks, and chocolate around bedtime, and avoiding nicotine and alcohol.

Make sure you create a sleep-conducive environment for yourself. You need to make sure the mattress you sleep on is well-fitting for your back. Your mattress shouldn't be too hard or too soft. The curve of your spine should be straight when you turn on your side or when you turn on your back. Also, the pillows that you use are very important. Your pillows should fit with the curvature of your neck. Some people find it helpful to place a pillow under their legs when they sleep because it eases lower back pressure and helps them sleep better. Also make sure the room temperature is comfortable.

You also need to sleep in a well-darkened room. Use eye covers if necessary. Also consider buying vertical blinds or room-darkening drapes that will block the early morning sunrays from coming into your room. It's important to sleep where it's quiet. This can be hard if you live near a highway or train tracks. In such cases, it might be a good idea to get earplugs. If you have a spouse who snores or there are other noises in your house, those earplugs will be very useful to you. Also, don't keep a television set in your bedroom, because you'll be tempted to watch it when you should be sleeping.

Sufficient sleep is important for both your mental and physical health. It says in Psalm 127:2, *"It is vain for you to rise up early, to sit up late, to eat the bread of sorrows: for so he giveth his beloved sleep."* God grants sleep to those He loves. Sufficient sleep is so important to have. When you make sure you get enough rest, you'll have new strength for the following day and better health overall.

Exercising Regularly

"Physical exercise has some value" (1 Timothy 4:8a, NLT).

It's interesting to note what Paul writes to Timothy here. He's saying that bodily exercise has some value. In the rest of the verse, he explains that godliness profits all things. But he does acknowledge that physical exercise is important. Physical exercise profits the body. The body is the shell in which our soul lives. It's also the temple of the Holy Spirit. That's why it is so important that we spend some time exercising our body.

Our bodies are made to move. Our bodies are made to exert energy. In the past, people would exert energy by working in the fields. But most of us in today's society are very sedentary. We would rather drive than walk somewhere, or take the elevator instead of the stairs. The majority of people today don't move around enough. That's why we need to exercise regularly.

But I don't encourage exercising as the main way to lose weight. The main way to lose weight is by eating properly and eating regularly. I lost over fifty pounds and Ljiljana lost thirty pounds within a six-month period. The way we did it was by changing our eating habits. That's a much better means of losing weight. (I'll discuss more about proper ways of losing weight at the end of this chapter.)

Exercise is important for strengthening our bones. It gives us energy and it strengthens our muscles so that we have more stamina. We should exercise about three to four times a week. This is an excellent stress reliever. There are various ways to exercise. You can go for a brisk walk every day for fifteen to twenty minutes or you can walk thirty to fifty minutes three times a week. Hippocrates said, "Walking is man's best medicine."[26] The ancients have realized the importance of exercise.

You can also go for a bike ride around the neighbourhood. Our family likes to do this, especially when warmer weather arrives. Or you can ride on a stationary bike. If you like to listen to music or sermons while you exercise, do it. That way, your mind will be occupied and you'll be able to exercise for thirty minutes or more.

Walking is man's best medicine.
– Hippocrates

You could also go to a gym. I find the gym very useful. There are a variety of things you can do at the gym. You can walk briskly on a treadmill. You can go on different types of bikes. Or you can do weightlifting. When you lift weights, your muscles become heated so they are exerting more energy. Usually, you burn more calories that way than by using a treadmill or bike. I would recommend, however, that you start exercising with a professional trainer for at least a few weeks, if you join a gym. That way, you'll learn how to use the equipment properly so you don't hurt yourself.

Another way to exercise is by engaging in sports. You could play basketball or hockey. Playing tennis or ping pong are other options. I like ping pong especially. I play it with my sons almost every day for one hour or longer. You can get involved in any sport you like and feel comfortable with. Choose something that you enjoy and that you will engage in on a weekly basis, and stick with it. Through exercise, you speed up your metabolism and burn calories. It's important that you sweat during your workouts, too, because sweating is a way of cleansing your body of toxins.

Detoxification

"And he said unto them, This kind can come forth by nothing, but by prayer and fasting" (Mark 9:29).

Let me share a funny story with you. There was a man who loved to eat sweets. Every time before he ate a piece of cake, he would pray, "In Jesus' name, all calories come out of this cake right now!" On one such occasion, a Christian brother heard him pray that prayer and said, "Brother, Jesus said in Matthew 17:21, *This kind cannot come out, but by prayer and fasting.*"

The above biblical passage is actually about the disciples who were trying to heal a person but couldn't because of their lack of faith. So Jesus said to them that, in order for healing to happen in that case, they needed to spend more time in prayer and they needed to fast. When we abstain from food for an extended period of time, our spiritual focus is sharper and clearer. Also, we don't use the energy of our bodies to digest our food, but rather we allow our bodies to heal themselves. Fasting is a practice seen both in the Old and New Testaments and even in today's church. It's not something new.

As I said, many sicknesses come as a result of toxins in our bodies. Toxins in our bodies create chronic fatigue, heart disease, memory loss, premature aging, all kinds of skin disorders, arthritis, hormone imbalance, anxiety, headaches, cancers, and many other diseases. "Junk foods and soft drinks con-

But to eat when you are sick is to feed your sickness.
– Hippocrates

tain dangerous additives, chemicals, and many are laced with excitotoxins, [which] are substances added to foods and beverages that literally stimulate neurons to death, causing brain damage of varying degrees."[27]

That's why we need to detoxify our bodies from the poisons that accumulate within us through the air, water, and food.

Our bodies are already created with organs that help us cleanse out toxins. Such organs include the liver, kidneys, colon, and lungs. We also cleanse our bodies through our urinary tracts. Another important detoxifier is our skin. The skin is considered the third kidney. As I said, it's so important that we sweat, because when we sweat we are eliminating toxins from our bodies. God has created our body in a way that it should heal itself. But aside from those detoxifying organs, we also have to take active measures to cleanse our bodies. And a good way to detoxify our bodies is to fast.

Hippocrates said, "But to eat when you are sick is to feed your sickness."[28] In other words, when you're sick, that's the time to stop eating and detoxify your body. Fasting is a great medicine for sicknesses. At the first symptom of any sickness, our action should be to go on a fresh juice fast, usually until we become well again. It's good practice to fast one weekend per month (unless you've been diagnosed with diabetes or cancer) and one entire week in the spring and one entire week in the fall. Sometimes extended fasts of three to six weeks are also exceptionally good, not only for our physical health but for our spiritual well-being. When we fast, we should completely eliminate caffeine, pop, and alcohol from our diets if we normally consume any of those things (hopefully none at all). Fasting rejuvenates our bodies and cleanses our system. And as we juice our vegetables during the fast, we are providing the best building fuel for our cells to be rejuvenated. When we juice, we are able to absorb ninety-two percent of the nutrients of the food, which is the highest level of nutrient absorption. The juice can almost go intravenously into the blood system.

When you're sick, that's the time to stop eating and detoxify your body. Fasting is a great medicine for sicknesses.

One of the hardest jobs that our bodies have is to digest the food we eat. It's even harder than going to work in the field for a whole day. As I mentioned, you may have noticed that sometimes after you've eaten a big, unhealthy meal, you feel tired and sleepy afterwards. You're not supposed to feel sleepy after you eat. Eating should give you energy. But the reason you feel tired is that your digestive system is working very hard to try to digest the unhealthy, dead food you just ate.

There are little villis in the colon and intestines. Those little villis are supposed to grab and absorb the nutrients from the food we eat. But when we eat unhealthy, dead foods, what happens is those foods clog up our colon and intestines and, through petrification, create a little wall so that those villis are not able to absorb the nutrients of our food, even when we eat healthy food. But when we fast, we are giving our bodies rest in order to cleanse themselves of all the unhealthy substances we've put into them, and those petrified walls within our intestines and colons literally crumble.

When we're not fasting, we need to add fibre to our diets because fibre also helps to get rid of toxins in our bodies. Fibre is found in all raw, plant-based foods. Think of fibre as an intestinal broom that sweeps things along in your colon so that you can have regular bowel movements to eliminate waste.

In the Bible, we read about various lengths of fasts. There are partial fasts, total fasts, juice fasts, etc. I find that juice fasts work the best. The first fresh vegetable juice fast Ljiljana and I went on lasted fifty-seven days, and we found that experience very helpful for our health. When you go on a fresh juice fast for that long, you lose a lot of weight and you improve your health in a tremendous way.

But I do not suggest going on a fast to lose weight, because once you stop the fast and go back to eating, you end up gaining the weight back. Fasting is a not a good method for losing weight and keeping it off. I'll discuss the right way to lose weight later on in this chapter. Fasting should be used primarily to cleanse your body of accumulated toxins.

When I fast, I replace my meals with freshly made vegetable juices. Instead of breakfast, I drink two kinds of juices. The first juice I drink has one handful of parsley, three sticks of celery, one piece of ginger, one handful of spinach, and two cucumbers, which adds up to two cups. The second juice I drink in the morning is carrot juice, which adds up to two cups as well.

Instead of lunch, I drink two cups of carrot juice mixed with two handfuls of spinach. Instead of supper, I drink two cups of carrot juice mixed with half a cucumber and one beet. As soon as I wake up and just prior to going to bed, I also drink one full cup of freshly squeezed lemon juice without any additives.

By following this method, both my wife and I have been able to fast as many as fifty-seven days in a row without feeling hungry. People think that when you go on a juice fast, you become weak and tired. But I find that I have more energy when I go on a juice fast. Since 1995, Ljiljana and I have gone on a juice fast several weeks at a time every year. As I said, the first one we went on lasted fifty-seven days in 1995 (I did another fifty-seven days of fresh juice fast in 2010 as well), but after that we've fasted for anywhere between three to six weeks each year, and it has served us well to cleanse ourselves from the toxins in our bodies.

Fresh vegetable juice fasts nourish our bodies. Making our own fresh fruits and vegetable juices is one of the wonderful ways we can bless our bodies with great health. One of the most important appliances in your kitchen should be the juicer, not the stove. So get a juicer and start juicing!

Another good thing to use for detoxification is an infrared sauna. An infrared sauna emits infrared radiant heat into the human body under your skin, whereas a regular sauna heats your body directly onto the

One of the most important appliances in your kitchen should be the juicer. So get a juicer and start juicing!

skin, which is why you cannot stand the heat in traditional saunas (which can heat up over ninety degrees Celsius, two hundred degrees Fahrenheit), as much as you could in an infrared sauna. Through infrared saunas, you experience far better and easier toxic elimination—up to three times more—which in turn strengthens the immune system.

But it's important that while we're detoxifying and cleansing our bodies, we also cleanse our spirits. In Ephesians 4:31–32 it says, *"Let all bitterness, and wrath, and anger, and clamour, and evil speaking, be put away from you, with all malice: And be ye kind one to another, tenderhearted, forgiving one another, even as God for Christ's sake hath forgiven you."*

Many sicknesses are caused by bitterness and grudges. Forgiveness is the antidote. So if we have any negative feelings toward anyone, we are to forgive him or her in the name of Jesus. In Matthew 6:14–15 Jesus said, *"For if ye forgive men their trespasses, your heavenly Father will also forgive you: But if ye forgive not men their trespasses, neither will your Father forgive your trespasses."* Forgiveness is so important for spiritual cleansing.

Taking Supplements

"But in the seventh year shall be a sabbath of rest unto the land, a sabbath for the LORD: thou shalt neither sow thy field, nor prune thy vineyard" (Leviticus 25:4).

We discussed earlier that we are to work six days and then rest on the seventh, which is the Sabbath day. Well, it's important to remember that we should treat our land the same way. The above verse is about the Sabbath of the land. In the previous verse, Leviticus 25:3, we read, *"Six years thou shalt sow thy field, and six years thou shalt prune thy vineyard, and gather in the fruit thereof."* According to these passages, not only should our bodies get rest, but the earth should rest every seven years.

Most of the food in North America is mass produced. We don't give our land rest; as a result, the ground loses its natural nutrients. Like our body, the ground needs to recharge. But when we constantly deplete the ground of its nutrients, the ground isn't able to pass along those nutrients to the fruits and vegetables we plant into it. There are some researchers who suggest that we lose up to fifty percent of nutrients in our foods because we don't let the ground rest.[29] Because of this, it's important to add some supplements to our diet, especially antioxidants.

Antioxidants are the enemies of the free radicals in our bodies. Free radicals create poisons (acidity) in our bodies. Those free radicals scavenge all the good nutrients in our bodies and destroy them. They also cause inflammation, and in-

It's important to add some supplements to our diet, especially antioxidants.

flammation causes all kinds of sicknesses. So we need to put antioxidants in our bodies in order to stop the harmful effects of free radicals.

The best way to take in nutrients (like vitamins and minerals) is through the food we eat on a daily basis. But more often than not, we don't eat the proper food and don't get sufficient nutrients from the food we eat. Supplements that should be used every day are (they are basically antioxidants): once a day multivitamins and chelated minerals, vitamin B complex, vitamin B3 or niacin, vitamin B6, vitamin B12, vitamin C, vitamin D, vitamin E, coenzyme Q10, selenium, zinc, calcium-magnesium (taken together), five percent HTP Hydroxythryptophan, EPA omega 3, cold-pressed borage oil, alpha-lipoic acid, and melatonin, which our brain already produces to help us relax.

At age forty and up, every woman should be taking at least some of these vitamins, and at age fifty at the latest, every man should be doing the same. You might think there is a cost involved in these, but there is even more cost involved in being sick. Also, if we need to we can always cut back on some other expenses like eating out, going to the movies, and buying new clothes in order to take care of our health first. Our health should take precedence over these and should be our major priority. In addition to taking those supplements, you should take advantage of the benefits found in stevia extract, green tea, dark chocolate, and herbal laxatives.

Proper Ways to Lose Weight

"I discipline my body like an athlete, training it to do what it should" (1 Corinthians 9:27a, NLT).

It's interesting to look at this verse and the context in which it is found. In 1 Corinthians 9:24 we read, *"Remember that in a race everyone runs, but only one person gets the prize. You also must run in such a way that you will win"* (NLT). In other words, Paul is encouraging the people of Corinth to engage in an activity with the purpose of winning. If you don't want to win, why participate?

Then he uses an illustration about athletes in verse 25a: *"All athletes practice strict self-control"* (NLT). There is no way you can win a prize without strict self-control. Then, in verse 26a, Paul wrote, *"So I run straight to the goal with purpose in every step"* (NLT). This is so important. You are to run toward your goal with purpose in every step, meaning every step you take should have your ultimate goal in mind. And in order to do that, you need to discipline your body, as we read in verse 27a.

> *There is no way we can reach our goal of optimum health if we don't discipline ourselves as to how we're handling our bodies.*

Weight loss is something that requires discipline. There is no way we can reach our goal of optimum health if we don't discipline ourselves as to how we're handling our bodies. Your body should be subject to the goals you have for it, which is to be for the glory of God. When your body is sick or overweight, you don't have vitality and energy to do much for God. According to Proverbs 23:21, *"For the drunkard and the glutton shall come to poverty: and drowsiness shall clothe a man with rags."*

Sometimes we take better care of our vehicles than our own bodies. We give our cars the fuel they need to run

> *Most diets don't work. What really works is a change of lifestyle.*

well. We change the oil regularly. We take our cars for tests whenever it's necessary. We do all that because we want to make sure our vehicles are in good condition, and we *should* take care of our cars. But what kind of fuel do we put into our bodies? Is the fuel we put into our bodies (water and food) going to cleanse and build our bodies or clog our bodies up?

According to 1 Corinthians 9:27, Paul was disciplining his body like an athlete; he was training it to do what it should. If you and I need to lose weight, you and I need to change our *lifestyles*.

Over sixty percent of North Americans are overweight.[30] People who are inventing new types of diets or weight loss programs are making billions of dollars. It seems overweight people often go on these diets, lose the weight, get off the diet, and then gain even more weight than what they started with. Most diets don't work. What really works is a change of lifestyle.

For most of our lives, my wife and I were slim. But after we had our third child in 1993, we started gaining weight. Then, for twelve years after that, we struggled with our weight. So for the first time in 1995, Ljiljana and I went on a juice fast for fifty-seven days, and we lost over fifty pounds. It was excellent! But then, within a year or two, we gained all of it back and even some more weight. It was very frustrating, but we still went on a juice fast every year, though for shorter periods of time. However, this time it wasn't for the purpose of weight loss. It was for the cleansing of toxins in our bodies.

Juice fasts are effective for weight loss, but not for keeping the weight off. The same is true for going on a diet. A lot of diets can help you lose weight, but when you get off the diet, what do you do? You often gain the weight back; sometimes you gain even more, so you go on another diet. Albert Einstein said, "The definition of insanity is doing the same thing over and over again and thinking you're going to get different results." You've got to change what you're doing if you want different results.

Eventually I got to a point where my heaviest weight was 243 pounds, and Ljiljana's heaviest weight was 210 pounds. So we tried to learn from the Word of God and from health books why we gained so much weight. We discovered that some of the reasons included stress related problems, eating the wrong foods, drinking the wrong drinks, not cleansing our bodies, and not giving our bodies enough nutrients.

So we started exercising at the end of 2005. I started exercising because I felt a lack of energy. As soon as I started exercising, I noticed that I gained energy. But the weight didn't go down. So Ljiljana and I started putting into practice some of the things we learned about food that we learned from the Word of God and various health books. When we changed what we ate, how much we ate, and what we drank, we started noticing a big difference. By eliminating the foods that were creating acidity in our bodies and adding alkaline foods to our diet, we started feeling less hungry and we started losing weight rapidly.

If you want to maintain the weight that you presently have, all you have to do is take in fifteen calories per pound of your weight. Let's say you're two hundred pounds. Multiply that by

> *"The definition of insanity is doing the same thing over and over again and thinking you're going to get different results."*
> *– Albert Einstein*

fifteen calories and you get three thousand. So in order to maintain your weight of two hundred pounds, you should be taking in three thousand calories a day.

But let's say you're two hundred pounds and you want to *lose* weight. You have to reduce your caloric intake to ten or twelve calories per pound, which is 2,000–2,400 calories a day. If you are two hundred pounds, you shouldn't be taking in any more than 2,000–2,400 calories a day if you want to lose weight. If you want to lose weight more rapidly, you could reduce your caloric intake even more. But you must do this carefully and the best way is to be under medical supervision during rapid weight loss. If you lose weight slowly by taking ten to twelve calories per pound, you could probably do that on your own without any problems. It is very important that you don't take fewer calories than you really need. The minimum calories that you should be consuming can be determined by following the rule of ten. Determine your ideal desired weight in pounds. Multiply it by ten, and that should be your minimum caloric intake if you are trying to maintain your ideal weight. That way, you will not go on binges as a result of malnutrition.

If you're overweight, it's so important to reduce your caloric intake. When people reduce their calories, they live longer. More than two thousand studies support the fact that a low calorie diet is an optimal program that can extend life by anywhere between thirty to fifty percent.[31]

My wife and I followed the above rule of ten. As I said, I lost over fifty pounds and my wife lost thirty pounds within a six-month period. We didn't do it because we accepted a diet plan, but because we made a *lifestyle change*.

Changing our lifestyle was how we lost all the weight. People sometimes ask us if it was hard. It wasn't hard at all, because we were losing weight while we were eating. Now we feel great! The only way you can maintain the weight is the way you worked on losing it through the reduction of your caloric intake. If you ensure that your plate is three-quarters raw or almost raw vegetables and is one-quarter cooked food, you will do well.

You may be wondering what we're doing to keep the weight off. Well, we keep the weight off by maintaining the lifestyle change that we've made. Ljiljana and I have made a lifestyle change. We've changed what we eat and we've reduced how much we eat. Because of that, we lost a considerable amount of weight in a short period of time. You can do the same! It's not hard. Just follow the instructions in this book and do what you need to do to get healthy! Keep at it and you'll get there!

Everything I've mentioned in this chapter is important to practice if we are to achieve natural healing. God has created fruits, vegetables, seeds, and water for us, and He intended for those things to be our main source of food. According to Ezekiel 47:12, our food is our medicine. There are powerful elements of healing in the very things that God created for us in nature. But it's up to us to take advantage of those healthy nutrients by putting them in our bodies. That's when we'll experience natural healing.

Now that I've thoroughly discussed how you can achieve natural healing through your actions and change of lifestyle, let's take a look at the importance of making positive confessions about your health and every other area of your life. Remember what I said earlier about the consequences of making wrongful confessions over your health? That is one of the three main reasons why Christians get sick. So let's now proceed to Chapter Five and explore the Word of God to discover how you can start making positive confessions over your life and experience the results of those confessions.

CHAPTER FIVE
Positive Confessions

"Death and life are in the power of the tongue: and
they that love it shall eat the fruit thereof"
(Proverbs 18:21).

In Proverbs 4:23 we read, *"Keep thy heart with all diligence; for out of it are the issues of life."* God is telling us that we should keep our hearts with all diligence (the heart is our inner person, the inner part of who we are). In other words, we should guard our hearts. We have to be careful about what comes through our eyes and ears into our hearts. Why? Because out of the heart comes the issues of life. What goes out of it is the source from which comes life itself.

In Proverbs 18:21 we read that the power of life and death is in our tongues. That's why we need to be careful about what goes into our hearts and out of our mouths. When you and I open our mouths and speak, we'll get the fruit of whatever our tongues are saying, whether it is life or death. Death in this case could mean real physical death. The power of that is in our tongues. Our confession is so important. It's the key to what happens in our lives.

Remember: this is not the doctrine of "name it and claim it." There are actions that need to be taken in order to claim what you've named. But positive confessions do play a major initial role in the type of outcome you receive. Let me share a story with you to illustrate the importance of speaking positively.

When you and I open our mouths and speak, we'll get the fruit of whatever our tongues are saying, whether it is life or death.

As you know, I lost over fifty pounds in about six months. When I was heavy, I had lots of little collections of fat around my stomach. Those collections of fat are tumours. A tumour is a precursor to cancer. There are tumours that actually lead to cancer and there are benign tumours. These collections of fat are benign tumours. They usually aren't a concern when they're around the stomach area. They become more of a concern when they're around the chest area. I have three little ones around my chest. When I went to the doctor, he said, "These little tumours around your chest are a concern."

I asked him, "What do you suggest?"

"You should do a biopsy," he said.

I shared this news with my mother, who lives in Europe. And when I shared this with her, she started crying. I said, "Why are you crying? You're the one who told me to go to the doctor. I went and this is what the doctor said. I believe I'm healthy."

She asked, "How do you know?"

"I read in the Bible that I'm healed," I answered. "I know the results of the biopsy will be good." And sure enough, when the report came back, everything was fine. Had the report been different, I would have still declared that by His stripes I am healed. Then I would have done whatever else I needed to do to change the situation, especially the things I spoke about in the previous chapter.

God wants to heal us, but He wants us to make positive confessions in our lives regardless of the report. Positive confessions are declarations that are in line with the Word of God. When we speak words that declare God's Word, we will receive exactly what we have spoken because those words will lead us to actions that will produce those results.

The Power of Your Tongue

"Even so the tongue is a little member, and boasteth great things. Behold, how great a matter a little fire kindleth!" (James 3:5).

Even though your tongue is such a small part of your body, it has great power over your life. It's like a little match that can spark and ignite a huge blaze. In James 3:6 we read, *"And the tongue is a fire, a world of iniquity: so is the tongue among our members, that it defileth the whole body, and setteth on fire the course of nature; and it is set on fire of hell."* So the tongue can be a very destructive instrument.

There is so much to learn about the power of the tongue. We need to learn about our tongues and about the task that each and every one of us has to master. We all have to know the power of our words and know how to use our words to bless and not tear down.

It says in James 3:8, *"But the tongue can no man tame; it is an unruly evil, full of deadly poison."* Even though we do not have the ability to control our tongues, God, who is within us, can. When we fill our hearts with the Word of God, our mouths (which always speak that which is in our hearts, according to Luke 6:45c) are going to speak the Word of God. That's when we will be able to tame our tongues.

> *We all have to know the power of our words and know how to use our words to bless and not tear down.*

We read in James 3:2, *"For in many things we offend all. If any man offend not in word, the same is a perfect man, and able also to bridle the whole body."* The words that come out of our mouths have control over our lives. If we know how to control what comes out of our mouths, we can control our whole bodies and curb our entire nature.

It says in Proverbs 18:20a, *"A man's belly shall be satisfied with the fruit of his mouth."* Our words are seeds. When we speak them out, we are planting those seeds. Eventually those seeds will produce a fruit, and eventually we will have to eat of that fruit. Then, in Proverbs 18:20b, it says, *"And with the increase of his lips shall he be filled."* So if we plant good seeds, we'll reap good fruit. If we plant evil seeds, we'll reap evil fruit. But regardless of whether the fruit is evil or good, we must be satisfied with it, meaning we must deal with the consequences of our words. That's why we have to be careful of the words we speak.

In Isaiah 57:19 we read, *"I create the fruit of the lips; Peace, peace to him that is far off, and to him that is near, saith the LORD; and I will heal him."* God is the guarantor of our words. God will bring to existence every word that we speak. What a powerful truth. If we speak a word of healing, we're planting a seed of healing. That means the fruit that will be produced will be the fruit of healing. Whatever we speak, God stands behind it and promises to create whatever we have spoken. In Psalm 138:2 we read, *"For thou hast magnified thy word above all thy name."* We see here that even God places high value on His own words. So we should value both His words and our words as well.

In Numbers 14, we read a very good example of how much power we have in our tongues. At the time, the Israelites were complaining in the wilderness. They complained that they were going to die in the desert. In Numbers 14:27–28 God said, *"How long shall I bear with this evil congregation, which murmur against me? I have heard the murmurings of the children of Israel, which they murmur against me. Say unto them, As truly as I live, saith the LORD, as ye have spoken in mine ears, so will I do to you."* In other words, God delivered their complaints to them just as they had spoken.

Even though your tongue is such a small part of your body, it has great power over your life.

In Numbers 14:29 we read, *"Your carcases shall fall in this wilderness; and all that were numbered of you, according to your whole number, from twenty years old and upward, which have murmured against me."*

God promised to bring about whatever the Israelites murmured to Him. And that's exactly what happened.

If you don't like the fruit that you are reaping or the life that you are living, you have to check your words. If you don't like the fruit you are reaping, it's probably because you have sown some bad seeds. So you just have to change the seed, meaning you have to change the words you have been speaking about your circumstances and start speaking some positive words that are in line with the Word of God.

Your Words Determine Your Destiny

"For by thy words thou shalt be justified, and by thy words thou shalt be condemned" (Matthew 12:37).

These were the words of the Lord Jesus Christ. It's amazing how much weight Jesus puts upon our words. I think we, as people, ought to learn to do the same—to put weight upon our words—because our words have tremendous power. Our words release faith in our lives.

In the German translation *Hoffnung fuer Alle*, this verse says, *"An euern Worten entscheidet sich eure Zukunft.* In English, this translates to, *"Upon your words, your destiny is determined."* If you want to experience failure, all you have to do is speak failure over yourself. If you want to be sick, just speak sickness over yourself. But if you want to be successful, you have to speak success over your life. And if you want to be healthy, you have to speak healing over your body. The words you speak will move you to a corresponding action and in such a way your words will determine the outcome of your life.

The human brain is an amazing organ. The brain represents about two percent of the entire weight of the body. Yet it uses about twenty to thirty percent of the body's energy. The brain contains one hundred billion neurons, which are nerve cells. There was a study done in 2006 in Paris, France, that showed that the broca's area of the brain (located in the inferior frontal gyrus of the frontal lobe) is the executive centre that manages and organizes behaviour. The broca's area is also known as the centre of the brain or the speech centre. The study suggests that when people speak, their words influence the neurons in their brains and those neurons begin working to bring about the things that they spoke.[32]

"Upon your words, your destiny is determined" (Matthew 12:37, German Translation)

For example, if you say, "I'm old," all the neurons in your brain begin working to prepare your body for old age and death. On the other hand, if you say, "I'm young," all the neurons begin working to give your body strength and vitality. The words that you speak are extremely influential to your life situations. This is confirmed in Proverbs 18:21: *"Death and life are in the power of the tongue: and they that love it shall eat the fruit thereof."*

That's why it's so important that when we open our mouths to speak, we speak what God says about our life situations. For example, when we're sick, we should speak what God says concerning healing. God says that by His stripes, we've been healed (1 Peter 2:24c). So that's what we should speak when we are sick. But we should not say so to others, especially if they are not believers. When they see your symptoms of sickness and you say that you are not sick, they will say to you that you're lying. It would be a lie in their own mind. But when we say it to ourselves, we are speaking prophetically, calling those things that are not as though they are (Romans 4:17). We are speaking what we want to see in our lives as an end result.

Even God Himself declares *"the end from the beginning"* (Isaiah 46:10a, NASB). And that's exactly how we speak when we speak in line with the Word of God, because God declares us as healthy. By His stripes we are healed (Isaiah 53:5b). When we speak in line with the Word of God, we release the power of God in our lives to work on our behalf and to accomplish the purpose for which He sends His Word (Jeremiah 1:12)—in this case, in terms of our healing. But in order to align our speech with the Word of God, we need to have the Word of

God within our hearts. We have to renew our minds with the Word so that we can renew our speech according to the Word (Romans 12:2).

What you say is an expression of what is in your heart, because out of the abundance of the heart the mouth will speak (Luke 6:45b). So you have power over your life through the words you say. This includes your salvation, healing, marriage, children, and finances. In Romans 10:9–10, it says that we receive salvation through what we say with our lips and what we believe in our hearts. The same would be true if we confess with our lips and believe in our hearts for the divine healing provided for us at the cross of Calvary. From a medical point of view, when we speak this positively we release positive neurons within our physical system that prompt a feeling of well-being to other neurons, which in turn speeds up our healthful recovery. But if you speak negatively about your life, you will only receive negative results. So if you have been speaking negatively about certain areas in your life, stop right now and start speaking positively in line with the Word of God. If you want something good to happen, you have to speak good things.

If you want to be sick, just speak sickness over yourself... If you want to be healthy, you have to speak healing over your body.

Even if you don't quite believe them in your heart, make those positive confessions anyway, because eventually (as you continue to speak them) your heart will begin to believe the words you say. According to Romans 10:17, faith comes from hearing and hearing through the Word of God. So when you and I start speaking the Word of God, in our case about divine healing on our behalf, that sound we hear out of our mouths can be heard through our hearing organs.

When we speak, we don't hear ourselves through our outer ears but through our inner ears. That is why when we listen to our pre-recorded speech our voice doesn't sound at all as we are accustomed to hearing it. But to other people it sounds very much like it, because they are used to hearing our voice through their outer ears. But when we speak, we hear ourselves through our inner ears, which are closer to our heart, and it actually helps us to gain faith in what we are saying sooner than if we just heard someone else talk about it. So it's important that you and I speak about our own well-being as God does in His Word. When we do that, the sound of the Word of God produces faith in our hearts, and then faith moves us to action, which in turn produces the result and the manifestation. As that happens, you will see the things you have confessed start to take place in your life. Your words have great power to shape your future.

Remember, in order to be saved you have to confess with your mouth that Jesus is Lord and believe in your heart that God raised Him from the dead (Romans 10:9). So in order to be healthy, you have to confess with your mouth and believe in your heart that you are healthy. Yes indeed, you can have what you say (Mark 11:23).

In Matthew 21:21–22 we read, *"Jesus answered and said unto them, Verily I say unto you, If ye have faith, and doubt not, ye shall not only do this which is done to the fig tree, but also if ye shall say unto this mountain, Be thou removed, and be thou cast into the sea; it shall be done. And all things, whatsoever ye shall ask in prayer, believing, ye shall receive."* In these passages, Jesus said that

> *If you doubt what you speak, you cannot receive what you desire.*

if you have faith in Him (meaning if you have trust and reliance upon His name) and you speak anything without doubting in your heart, whatever you speak will come to pass.

The word "doubt" in Greek is *diakrite,* which means to question through and through. If you doubt what you speak, you cannot receive what you desire. But if you don't doubt that God has given you divine power to speak and cause things to happen, you will receive whatever you speak. Isn't that powerful?

According to Matthew 21:22, if you have a mountain in your life, you can speak to that mountain and command it to be thrown into the sea. In this case, your mountain may be a sickness, perhaps brought on by your own actions or a spirit of sickness. It says in Isaiah 53:5c, *"With his stripes we are healed."* You can declare this verse over your life. God wants you to speak to that mountain of sickness and say, "Sickness, you do not belong to me! My body is the temple of the Holy Spirit. Sickness, I command you to leave my body in Jesus' name, because by His stripes I am healed!"

But then God might require you to change your lifestyle in order to better your health, such as drinking more water, eating healthier foods, exercising, forgiving someone who has offended you, and everything else I discussed in the previous chapters. Now you have to start walking in obedience to God's Word and start *doing* what you need to do to improve your health. But the first step to removing any mountain in your life is speaking to it, because your words move you to action and in such a way they determine your destiny.

Remember what I said in the first chapter about the steps required to take you from words to destiny? Let us review them. First, it starts with your words. Then your words become thoughts, which influence your emotions. Your emotions move you to make decisions, which results in action. Continuous action develops into habits. Then your habits determine your character, and your character determines your destiny. It's amazing how it all started with your words. You have the power to determine your destiny in any area of your life, and it starts with the words you speak. What you say comes from the depths of your heart and it has a direct influence on your actions. Let us do what God does and declare *"the end from the beginning"* (Isaiah 46:10a, NASB). That's why you and I should train our tongues so that the words that come out of our mouths become lined up with the Word of God. As it says in Colossians 3:16a, *"Let the word of Christ dwell in you richly in all wisdom."*

Speak Words of Life

"It is the spirit that quickeneth; the flesh profiteth nothing: the words that I speak unto you, they are spirit, and they are life" (John 6:63).

If we can relate God's Spirit to the words of Jesus, we can understand that evil spirits are connected to the words of Satan—meaning, if the words of God are spirit and life, then the words of Satan are spirit and death. So it's obvious

If the words of God are spirit and life, the words of Satan are spirit and death.

that evil spirits are related to satanic words, which are words that are contrary to the Word of God. The moment we accept Satan's words and believe those words as truth, we will receive what those negative words are saying.

Let's say, for example, you become sick and start believing that you will never get better. According to Isaiah 53:5, you are healed by the stripes of Jesus. But if you believe that you're always going to be sick, you'll always be sick. If you choose to speak and believe the words of Satan, you are going to receive what Satan speaks to you. On the other hand, if you choose to speak and believe the Word of God (the word of life), you will receive what the Word promises, which is life.

One day, a lady called me after watching one of our programs and said, "I am cursed." I knew she was a believer. She actually worked for several reputable Christian organizations. At this point, she was with her second husband and had four children, and she was struggling emotionally, spiritually, financially, and in every other way.

So I asked her, "Did God tell you that you're cursed?"

"Oh no, God didn't tell me that," she answered.

"Did you read it in the Bible?"

"No, I didn't read it in the Bible."

"If you didn't read it in the Bible and God didn't call you cursed, where do you think those words came from?" I asked.

"Oh, I don't know. But I'm so desperate."

I said, "If those words didn't come from God or His Word, they must have come from the devil." She was surprised to hear this, but she agreed.

So when you and I speak words that are contrary to what the Word of God says, we are speaking words of death. That's why it's so important to do what Joshua 1:8 says: *"This book of the law shall not depart out of thy mouth; but thou shalt meditate therein day and night, that thou mayest observe to do according to all that is written therein: for then thou shalt make thy way prosperous, and then thou shalt have good success."* We need the Word of God more than anything else. We need to speak it, meditate therein, and act upon it.

It says in Colossians 3:16, *"Let the word of Christ dwell in you richly in all wisdom; teaching and admonishing one another in psalms and hymns and spiritual songs, singing with grace in your hearts to the Lord."* There is nothing that can bring peace into your heart like the Word of God. Read the entirety of Psalm 119 and you'll learn about the many benefits of the Word of God.

If we speak words of life, we will prolong our lives.

Why should we speak words of life? Well, if we speak words of life, we will prolong our lives. We read in Psalm 34:12–13, *"What man is he that desireth life, and loveth many days, that he may see good? Keep thy tongue from evil, and thy lips from speaking guile."* God created each and every one of us with a desire in our hearts to live long and healthy lives. So it's not just a desire to live long; it's a desire to live well, too.

Psalm 34:12–13 teaches us that if we want to live long and well, we shouldn't allow our tongues to say anything evil. That's so important to remember. Keep in mind what

The words we store in our hearts are the key to our destiny, particularly when our words go from our mind to our hearts and are bridged by our mouths.

Proverbs 18:21 said: *"Death and life are in the power of the tongue: and they that love it shall eat the fruit thereof."* So the power of life and death are found in the power of the tongue. That's why we need to be careful of what our tongues speak.

If we want to live long and well, we have to remember that our tongues and actions have tremendous power over our lives. The majority of people who live short lives often do so because of the words they speak and the things they do. They usually say and do things that are contrary to the Word of God, things that are evil. That's why they live short lives. On the other hand, people who live long and fruitful lives are the ones who speak and do what the Word of God says. So our speech and actions will determine the outcome of our lives.

I have six children and I teach them the Word of God every day. Ever since they were born, they've been hearing the Word of God from me. Now they know over four hundred verses by heart. Even Elisabeth, who is ten years old, knows about one hundred verses by heart. Just recently, she learned Psalm 91. Now she knows Psalm 91, Psalm 103:1–5, Deuteronomy 28:1–14, Habakkuk 3:19, the Ten Commandments, and 1 Corinthians 13.

In addition to that, all my children are reading the Bible. I make sure they read the Bible every day. My daughter Elisabeth has read the Bible once through. My son Joshua, who is fourteen years old, has read the Bible seven times from cover to cover. My son Peter, who is seventeen, has read the Bible nine times from cover to cover. My daughter Sara, who is twenty, has read the Bible eleven times from cover to cover. My oldest son, David, who is eighteen, has read the Bible twenty times through. I believe the Word of God is the greatest thing they will be taking out of my home. Those words are spirit and life (John 6:63).

I wrote a book entitled *Bless Your Children to Succeed*, and one of the endorsements in it reads, "Slobodan and Ljiljana have some of the most well-adjusted, happy, and productive kids I've ever met in my life. I guess what they're doing is working. You can't do better than that!" That endorsement came from a businessman who said he'd like to hire my children as soon as they grow up. All of my children are honour students at the current time and they help us at home and with the ministry. And it's because of the Word of God in their hearts.

The words we store in our hearts are the key to our destiny, particularly when our words go from our mind to our hearts and are bridged by our mouths. When we open our mouths to speak, those words eventually move us into actions which produce results in our lives. That's why we need to speak words of spirit and life; we need to speak the Word of God.

Your Personal Confession

"Heal me, O LORD, and I shall be healed; save me, and I shall be saved: for thou art my praise" (Jeremiah 17:14).

Positive Bible-based confessions are important if you are to achieve any kind of success. Your words have so much power over your life. If you want to make today the beginning of your journey from sickness to health, I encourage you to make the following confession right now and on a daily basis:

> "My heavenly Father and Lord Jesus Christ, I commit my life right now to a healthy lifestyle today and every day of my life. I will only eat healthy food, and I will prepare only healthy meals for my family. I will treat my body as the temple of the Holy Spirit. I will keep my body healthy and cleansed by feeding it with essential life nutrients. In addition, I commit myself to exercising my body and strengthening my muscles and bones. I will bring my body under the subjection of my spirit and mind.
>
> I will commit to do what is best for my body, which is my living sacrifice that I present to You (Romans 12:1), so that the house in which You live will be holy

and acceptable to You. From now on, I'm going to see my body as a gift that You have given me. I'm not going to abuse it any longer, but I will nurture, nourish, and use it to bring glory to You. I do not belong to myself. I confess with my lips and trust in my heart that by Your stripes I am healed, right now. I belong to You, for I've been bought by the precious blood of Jesus. In Jesus' mighty name, Amen!"

My Personal Prayer for You

If you've made the above confession, congratulations! You're already on the road to success in your health. Speaking words of faith is the first step toward receiving your healing. Now that you've made your personal confession, let me join my faith with yours and trust God for divine healing to take place in your body.

"Father, in the name of Jesus I lift up to You every person who is reading this book and has made their personal confession regarding their health. It is not Your will for Your children to be sick. So in the name of Jesus, I command every sickness and disease to leave my brothers' and sisters' bodies right now. You foul spirit of sickness, leave his body and leave her body now in the name of Jesus Christ! You have no authority, no power, and no dominion to attach yourself to my brother and sister. So, spirit of sickness, go in the name of Jesus! I speak healing into my brother and sister. May they be healed from the crowns of their heads down to the soles of their feet!

Now, Father, I pray that You cover my brothers and sisters in the precious blood of Your Son. I pray that You will encourage them to stretch out by faith to re-

120

ceive their healing, and I pray that You will teach them and motivate them to make the necessary changes to live a long and healthy life just as You desire for them to live. Thank you, Lord, for healing my brother and sister in Jesus' mighty name, Amen!"

I encourage you now to agree with my prayer and say, "Yes, Lord, I receive it now. I receive my healing. I receive my deliverance." Now begin to do what you couldn't do before. Stretch out by faith. You've already received your healing. It doesn't matter what your symptoms may be telling you. Even if a symptom persists, don't let go of the healing that God has given you. Continue to stand upon the Word of God that you are healed and act upon that Word!

CONCLUSION

I trust that you have made the positive confession that I included in the last chapter and that you have agreed with my prayer for you about your healing. I trust that you will take hold of that which God has already provided for you through the sacrifice of Jesus Christ on the cross at Calvary. Salvation is yours, so you can take it. Healing is yours, so you can take it. If you don't take salvation, you can't have it. If you don't take healing, you can't have that, either.

It says in Romans 10:9–10, *"That if thou shalt confess with thy mouth the Lord Jesus, and shalt believe in thine heart that God hath raised him from the dead, thou shalt be saved. For with the heart man believeth unto righteousness; and with the mouth confession is made unto salvation."* Do you see how the confession of your mouth and the belief of your heart are both important elements for receiving salvation? We are to speak salvation with our mouths and we are to believe in our hearts that we are saved in order to be saved. Sometimes it takes time for the words of salvation to go from the mind to the heart. That is the longest journey there is. But the bridge between the two is the mouth, so start speaking words in line with the Word of God.

The same actions are required in order to receive our healing. We know that God healed in the Old Testament. We know that Jesus healed in the New Testament. We know the apostles engaged in preaching and healing, and we know that we are to engage in preaching and healing as well. We know that health is a blessing while sickness is a curse. We know that God doesn't want us to be sick. If He did, He would have said so. But He has never said that He wants us to be sick. God wants us to be healthy.

So you and I have to go to God in prayer and confess with our lips and trust in our hearts that by His stripes we are healed. We have to declare it like we declared our salvation. We have to confess with our mouths that Jesus is our Healer, and we have to believe with our hearts that He will heal us. I want to encourage you to do that right now.

If there is a sickness in your body, put your hand over that part of your body and declare yourself healed in the name of Jesus. Speak to every virus, every infection, every cancerous tumour, and every sick cell to die in the name of Jesus. God wants you to be healed. He wants you to live long and well. Whatever you were not able to do before, I encourage you to start doing it right now. God can heal you instantaneously, or it could take time. He is sovereign, but He certainly will not fail. So take hold of the Word of God. Speak the Word, believe it, and allow God to perform His supernatural healing in you.

But keep in mind that you may also be required to do certain things to receive your healing and continue walking in divine health. A lot of people who came to Jesus for healing were sick because they were possessed by the devil. But many people today are not sick because the devil has possessed them. They're sick because they've abused the natural laws that God has put in place.

For example, instead of putting living, alkaline food in their bodies, they're putting poisonous, dead food in their bodies. Death will not bring life. Only living food can bring life. It's important that you learn how you can make a lifestyle change in order to walk in divine health. Start with this book. Then do more research by using other books. And don't forget to use the Bible. Learn how you can change your lifestyle, because God will not do it for you. If you need to lose weight, God will not eat healthy and exercise for you. You have to do it.

Believe me, once you learn about all the harmful effects of toxic foods, you will not want to feed yourself with dead food any longer. I remember in my younger years, I loved French fries. I would always order a second portion of French fries instead of dessert. Now I can't stand French fries because of the oil and fat content. French fries have no nutritional value, so I will not eat them anymore. I've worked hard to eliminate toxins from my body. Why would I want to put more in?

In 1 Corinthians 6:19–20 we read, *"Know ye not that your body is the temple of the Holy Ghost which is in you, which ye have of God, and ye are not your own? For ye are bought with a price: therefore glorify God in your body, and in your spirit, which are God's."* Our bodies do not belong to us because we have been bought for a price.

We read in Romans 12:1, *"I beseech you therefore, brethren, by the mercies of God, that ye present your bodies a living sacrifice, holy, acceptable unto God, which is your reasonable service."* According to Leviticus 1–7, the sacrifices that the Israelites brought had to be without spot or blemish. So we need to give God a body that He can live in, a body that is without spot or blemish. In 1 Peter 1:19, we read that we were redeemed *"with the precious blood of Christ, as of a lamb without blemish and without spot."*

Your body is not your own; it belongs to God. So you shouldn't give your body whatever it wants—you should give your body what it *needs* to be healthy. Honour God in your body, and for as long you live use your body as a healthy home for the Spirit of God to dwell in. I encourage you to use the health plan of God and experience God's healing secrets. Be healthy! Be strong! Follow God's Word! Do your part! And you will walk in divine health.

ELIZABETH'S MIRACLE HEALING STORY

written by Ljiljana Krstevski

Years ago, I had a miscarriage, and those of you who have had miscarriages yourself know what it's like. It was the first time I lost a baby and I went through a valley of depression. But praise God, because He took me out of that valley and back into His joy. Soon after that, I became pregnant again.

One day, we were going in for a routine ultrasound. After the picture was taken, the specialist told me that it did not look good. This really shocked me because we already had four healthy children. But the specialist couldn't tell me what the problem was. He had to talk to his colleagues first, just to be sure.

I had to wait for three days, knowing that it was bad. Finally, I called him and he told me that the baby had an abdominal growth and this abdominal growth could cause cystic fibrosis. Then the doctor explained that this disease was genetically passed on and there was nothing the medical community could do.

He went on to tell me that babies with cystic fibrosis can live up to four years of age, but very few go on to live longer. The lungs and the stomach don't function properly and everything fills up with mucous. It is a 24-hour per day battle just for breath. You never know when, day or night, the attacks will become so bad that the child chokes on his or her own mucous. Then the baby is gone. That's how it usually goes, the doctor said.

I started to cry and thought, *How come? Why didn't it show up somewhere else in the family if they say it is genetic? It should have appeared somewhere else. How come, God?* But we cannot fight with God, can we? He has our lives in His hands. It wasn't long before my husband and I had nowhere else to go but on our knees before the Lord. Like little children, we prayed to the Lord, calling upon His mighty name. We also sent out prayer requests, asking our brothers and sisters in the Lord to unite with us in prayer for the healing of our baby.

One day, as I was feeling discouraged, the Lord reminded me of when we were in the Balkans during a missions trip. After a church meeting, a young pregnant lady came to the altar asking for prayer. She shared that the doctor had told her that the blood was impure and that she would most likely lose the baby. I remember some of us ladies were praying and crying out like little children asking God to touch her body, cleanse her blood, and spare her baby.

A week and a half later, this woman shared a wonderful testimony with me. She said that the doctor did another check-up and her blood was pure; the baby was just fine! Thinking back to that story, I then cried out for my own baby, *"God Almighty, would you heal my baby, too?"*

One day, I heard God's voice deep in my heart, saying, "It is done. Stop praying and start praising Me. Give Me thanks!" I had never heard anything like that before, but I knew that it was the Lord. Months later, I was called back for another ultrasound. The doctor took both ultrasound pictures, the one from last time and now this new one, and examined them. Then he said, "I can't find it. It isn't here." When I heard the doctor say that to my husband, I shouted, *Praise the Lord!* I didn't care who was around!

Right away, my husband started evangelizing. He said, "Doctor, did you know that hundreds of people have been praying for this baby to be healed?" When the doctor heard the word "prayer," he took another look at the ultrasound pictures. He then said, "Something has worked." But really, that *something* was *someone!* It was Jesus. He is real and He is alive!

On April 3, 2000, I was rushed to the hospital. To my surprise, but not God's, the doctor on duty that day was my own gynaecologist, Dr. Lamont. He ended up delivering my baby! We had a healthy baby girl, whom we named Elisabeth Lilyana Krstevski. On one of our weekly family meetings, it was Elisabeth who gave us the idea for the title of this book, *God's Healing Secrets*.

Through this experience, God has brought us so much closer to Him to really see Him as our only source. Just like little children, let us call upon God for everything. He's on our side. Our Daddy can do anything!

THE WORD OF LIFE

written by Sara Rozalina Krstevski

Looking at the precious bundle in her arms, Ljiljana Krstevski's heart was full of happiness. Deborah Faith, her third daughter and long-awaited sixth child, was born on July 13, 2010.

Thinking back on the difficulty of the last stage of pregnancy, Ljiljana was glad that it was over.

"In the last trimester, I was starting to have breathing problems," said Ljiljana. "I went to the doctor and got a puffer because he thought I had asthma."

On July 12, Ljiljana went for her regular check-up at the hospital. The doctor found her blood pressure to be pretty high and wanted to induce the delivery right there and then, two weeks before the due date.

Deborah came out alive and healthy.

"If the blood pressure was due to the pregnancy, the doctor said that it would be gone within two hours to a week," said Ljiljana.

But the problem wasn't going away. So the doctor gave her Trandate, a beta blocker medication, to help lower her blood pressure in the hospital.

Ljiljana and Deborah came home on July 15.

As the hours passed, Ljiljana's breathing became more laboured and painful.

"The medication seemed to be exasperating my situation rather than helping it," said Ljiljana.

The next day, her husband Slobodan brought her to the clinic where her breathing became even more painful and Ljiljana could barely speak.

The doctor ordered for an ambulance immediately.

"They didn't know what it was, but it was clearly seen that I was barely breathing, walking, or talking," said Ljiljana.

During that half-hour ride in the ambulance, a spiritual battle ensued.

"The lady gave me an oxygen mask and as I tried to breathe in, the air stopped partway inside of me. It was like a wall blocking the air from entering my lungs," said Ljiljana. "I cried to the lady for help, but she could give no assistance."

Ljiljana was suffocated to the brink of death and the invisible wall blocking the air from entering the lungs was becoming thicker and thicker.

Then Ljiljana heard a voice inside her head. *You're going to die.* Ljiljana tried breathing again, each effort as painful as a piercing knife. *Maybe you should have stayed at home and died with your family around you.* Ljiljana tried to ignore the taunting voice.

Her energy running out, she was at the point of giving up.

Ljiljana again cried to the nurse, "Please help me." Getting no response, Ljiljana turned to God and cried in her spirit, "Lord, please help me!"

"As soon as I called out to God, something happened. My spiritual eyes saw myself lying there in the ambulance. I saw the substance that was clogging my lungs coming out of my throat like a bubbling water fountain towards the sky," Ljiljana tearfully recalled. "Along with that substance were words."

Those words reminded her of God's power. *I will not die but live and tell about your glory... The Lord is my strength and refuge... I will praise the Lord and He will fight my battles.*

Soon after that, the ambulance arrived in the emergency room and they brought Ljiljana to the attention of several doctors and nurses right away.

"As soon as I saw the people around me, I told them to help me because I was starting to choke," Ljiljana recalled.

The doctors were huddled together, wondering what to do and what was going on.

"Their heads put together like that reminded me of a war situation room where generals discuss what the next step in the battle is," said Ljiljana. "And it really was a battle. A spiritual one. And I was hanging on to life."

Decisions had to be made quickly and one doctor knew what to do.

"I realized once again the importance of the Word of God in my life," said Ljiljana. "It is so important for us believers to read the Word and memorize it and store it in our hearts."

Ljiljana also explains how she insists that her children quote and memorize Scriptures every month. "It's the greatest gift that the Father has given to us. It is a powerful weapon," said Ljiljana. "It is life for those who find it and healing to our flesh. I thank the Lord for what He has done for me."

Ljiljana will continue to live and tell the story of God's goodness in her life.

CURE FROM PROSTATE CANCER

written by Sara Rozalina Krstevski

Sitting in the comfort of his brown couch, Slobodan Krstevski looked at ease. Running his fingers through his brown hair, he looked ready to relate his story about prostate cancer.

"It was when I was around fifty when I noticed that I was urinating blood," said Slobodan. "Knowing that wasn't normal, my wife Ljiljana and I went to the hospital the same day to get some blood tests done."

The doctors made a diagnosis that the bleeding must have been a result of urinary tract infection.

"The doctors didn't think it was anything serious, so I went ahead with the planned family trip to a conference in Nashville," said Slobodan. "After listening to a speech given by the then-presiding U.S. President George W. Bush, I went on a bathroom break and noticed that I was urinating blood again."

Once Slobodan returned to Canada, he went for a string of blood and urine tests to see if the cause of the blood was urinary tract infection or something more serious.

"All the results were negative. So I insisted on seeing a specialist, and a urologist directed me to have a PSA test, which is a prostate cancer marker," said Slobodan. "The PSA reading was elevated at 5.89, which was concerning, according to the doctor, considering that the normal reading is less than four."

Because of this result, the urologist suggested a biopsy of the prostate.

"On June 4, 2008, they took ten cores from my prostate, and six of them were cancerous," said Slobodan. "The doctor told me that since the cancer was severe, I was at risk of dying during the next ten to fifteen years if I didn't do anything."

Slobodan and Ljiljana, both holding firm to their Christian faith and God's Word, decided to listen to the Lord's report over the doctor's report.

"We repeated Romans 4:17 over my body and declared healing of my prostate in Jesus' name and by His blood," said Slobodan. "We were calling things that were not as though they were."

Knowing that speaking the Word was important to get his faith stirred, Slobodan also knew that true faith also brought a corresponding action. He knew he had to change his lifestyle in order to bring about healing in his body.

"A friend of mine from Alberta told me about a medical clinic in Tijuana, Mexico, where they practice an integrated approach to treating cancer," said Slobodan. "This means they use alternative medicine through natural means and they use partial standard medicine."

Slobodan went there for three weeks of treatments, which required a lifestyle change.

"Besides the natural treatments, I was also following the advice that they gave me in what I was supposed to be eating," said Slobodan. "They told me to stop eating white bread, white flour, white pasta, and not to eat any sweets, because cancer feeds on sugar."

This period of time was hard on the family as Slobodan was absent a lot from home for different treatments and endless tests.

"While there, I took my faith and my Bible. They were a great comfort to me," said Slobodan. "The only thing that alternative doctors can do is alleviate pain and extend life, but they cannot cure cancer, because only God above does the curing."

Later that year, in October, Slobodan went for an abdominal CT scan and total bone scan. There was no evidence of metastasized disease anywhere.

"The results were negative, which meant that I had no more cancer," said Slobodan. "Later that month, I went for another blood test reading of the PSA level and the reading was only 1.57, which was better than it had been for the last several years."

Whatever tests Slobodan took, the results for cancer were negative.

"My urologist thought that I was using some medicine to reduce the PSA level," said Slobodan. "I told him that the only thing I had used were some natural herbs, like saw palmetto, which had been prescribed by my doctors in Mexico."

So as far as the Krstevskis knew, the cancer was completely gone. However, Slobodan asked for another biopsy to be done (July 20, 2009) and discovered that even though the natural herbal remedy was reducing the PSA level to normal, it had not removed the cancer: nine out of ten cores were cancerous.

"I went to Florida in early September that year to be seen by Dr. Don Colbert, a well-known physician in the Christian community, and he advised me to proceed with High-Intensity Focused Ultrasound (HIFU), which I did the following month," said Slobodan. "It's a two- to three-hour non-surgical medical procedure that cooks the prostate tissue with ultrasound heat."

Now that Slobodan's prostate tissue has been cooked, the cancer in the prostate has also been cooked and destroyed. This was confirmed by the third biopsy in June 3, 2010, when all five cores taken were cancer free, and an MRI-S was done on August 26, 2010.

Slobodan's cure from prostate cancer was a tough road, but God was with him all the way. Slobodan was healed from prostate cancer because he confessed the Word with faith and because he did what he had to do to get well.

You can do the same today. Start *believing* in God's healing power now, begin taking corresponding *actions* based on the Word of God, and you will begin to see the positive results in your own health.

SCRIPTURES ON HEALING

The Word of God is so powerful when it is in our hearts, upon our lips, and in our actions. For that reason, I've included various Scriptures on healing that I know will be of encouragement to you. I've also included a powerful confession before each Scripture reference that you can make in order to strengthen your faith.

He's the Lord God who heals me because I diligently read, meditate upon, practice, and speak the Word of God. (Exodus 15:26)
"If you will listen carefully to the voice of the LORD your God and do what is right in his sight, obeying his commands and laws, then I will not make you suffer the diseases I sent on the Egyptians; for I am the LORD who heals you" (NLT).

He takes sicknesses away from me through the healthy food I eat and the water I drink. (Exodus 23:25)
"And ye shall serve the LORD your God, and he shall bless thy bread, and thy water; and I will take sickness away from the midst of thee."

He keeps me from diseases. (Deuteronomy 7:15)

"And the LORD will protect you from all sickness. He will not let you suffer from the terrible diseases you knew in Egypt, but he will bring them all on your enemies!" (NLT).

I will choose life in accordance to His Word. (Deuteronomy 30:19)

"I call heaven and earth to witness this day against you that I have set before you life and death, the blessings and the curses; therefore choose life, that you and your descendants may live" (AMP).

All of His promises for me are good and will come to pass. (Joshua 21:45)

"All of the good promises that the LORD had given Israel came true" (NLT).

God will give me a long life. (Psalm 91:16)

"With long life will I satisfy him and show him My salvation" (AMP).

I will bless the Lord, for He will heal all my diseases. (Psalm 103:1–5)

"Bless the LORD, O my soul: and all that is within me, bless his holy name. Bless the LORD, O my soul, and forget not all his benefits: Who forgiveth all thine iniquities; who healeth all thy diseases; Who redeemeth thy life from destruction; who crowneth thee with lovingkindness and tender mercies; who satisfieth thy mouth with good things; so that thy youth is renewed like the eagle's."

He heals me with His Word. (Psalm 107:20)

"He sent his word, and healed them, and delivered them from their destructions."

I will not die, but I will live. (Psalm 118:17)

"I shall not die, but live, and declare the works of the LORD."

I pay attention to His Word, for it brings health to all of my flesh. (Proverbs 4:20–23)

"My son, attend to my words; incline thine ear unto my sayings. Let them not depart from thine eyes; keep them in the midst of thine heart. For they are life unto those that find them, and health to all their flesh. Keep thy heart with all diligence; for out of it are the issues of life."

He blots out my transgressions. (Isaiah 43:25–26)

"I, even I, am He Who blots out and cancels your transgressions, for My own sake, and I will not remember your sins. Put Me in remembrance [remind Me of your merits]; let us plead and argue together. Set forth your case, that you may be justified (proved right)" (AMP).

By His stripes I am healed. (Isaiah 53:5)

"But he was wounded for our transgressions, he was bruised for our iniquities: the chastisement of our peace was upon him; and with his stripes we are healed."

He will restore my health and heal me. (Jeremiah 30:17a)

"I will give you back your health and heal your wounds, says the LORD." (NLT).

I am strong! (Joel 3:10)

"Beat your plowshares into swords, and your pruninghooks into spears: let the weak say, I am strong."

God will mightily bless me in my work when I tithe. (Malachi 3:10)

"Bring all the tithes (the whole tenth of your income) into the storehouse, that there may be food in My house, and prove Me now by it, says the Lord of hosts, if I will not open the windows of heaven for you and pour you out a blessing, that there shall not be room enough to receive it" (AMP).

Jesus is willing to make me well by curing me. (Matthew 8:2–3)

"And behold, a leper came up to Him and, prostrating himself, worshipped Him, saying, Lord, if You are willing, You are able to cleanse me by curing me. And He reached out His hand and touched him, saying, I am willing; be cleansed by being cured. And instantly his leprosy was cured and cleansed" (AMP).

The authority is mine to bind and loose things on this earth. God answers my prayers. (Matthew 18:18–19)

"Verily I say unto you, Whatsoever ye shall bind on earth shall be bound in heaven: and whatsoever ye shall loose on earth shall be loosed in heaven. Again I say unto you, That if two of you shall agree on earth as touching any thing that they shall ask, it shall be done for them of my Father which is in heaven."

By faith in what I say, I can move mountains. I will have whatever I pray for. (Mark 11:23–24)

"For verily I say unto you, That whosoever shall say unto this mountain, Be thou removed, and be thou cast into the sea; and shall not doubt in his heart, but shall believe that those things which he saith shall come to pass; he shall have whatsoever he saith. Therefore I say unto you, What things soever ye desire, when ye pray, believe that ye receive them, and ye shall have them."

Miracles will follow me because I believe in the name of the Lord Jesus Christ and His Word. (Mark 16:17–18)

"These signs will accompany those who believe: They will cast out demons in my name, and they will speak new languages. They will be able to handle snakes with safety, and if they drink anything poisonous, it won't hurt them. They will be able to place their hands on the sick and heal them" (NLT).

God hears me because I worship Him and I do His will. (John 9:31)

"We know that God does not listen to sinners; but if anyone is God-fearing and a worshipper of Him and does His will, He listens to him" (AMP).

I will have and enjoy life with an overflowing abundance. (John 10:10)
"The thief comes only in order to steal and kill and destroy. I came that they may have and enjoy life, and have it in abundance (to the full, till it overflows)" (AMP).

The Spirit of God, who raised Jesus from the dead, is living within me. (Romans 8:11)
"And if the Spirit of Him Who raised up Jesus from the dead dwells in you, [then] He who raised up Christ Jesus from the dead will also restore to life your mortal (short-lived, perishable) bodies through His Spirit Who dwells in you" (AMP).

God will fulfill all of His promises to me. (2 Corinthians 1:20)
"For all the promises of God in him are yea, and in him Amen, unto the glory of God by us."

Every stronghold in my life is broken by the knowledge of the Word of God and the Lordship of Christ. (2 Corinthians 10:4–5)
"For the weapons of our warfare are not physical [weapons of flesh and blood], but they are mighty before God for the overthrow and destruction of strongholds, [Inasmuch as we] refute arguments and theories and reasonings and every proud and lofty thing that sets itself up against the [true] knowledge of God; and we lead every thought and purpose away captive into the obedience of Christ (the Messiah, the Anointed One)" (AMP).

Christ has redeemed me from the curse and given me the blessings of Abraham. (Galatians 3:13–14)
"But Christ has rescued us from the curse pronounced by the law. When he was hung on the cross, he took upon himself the curse for our wrongdoing. For it is written in the Scriptures, 'Cursed is everyone who is hung on a tree.' Through the work of Christ Jesus, God has blessed the Gentiles with the same blessing he

promised to Abraham, and we Christians receive the promised Holy Spirit through faith" (NLT).

I stand firm against all the tricks of the devil, for I am wearing the armour of God: truth, the gospel of peace, righteousness, salvation, and the Word of God. (Ephesians 6:10–17)

"In conclusion, be strong in the Lord [be empowered through your union with Him]; draw your strength from Him [that strength which His boundless might provides]. Put on God's whole armour [the armour of a heavy-armed soldier which God supplies], that you may be able successfully to stand up against [all] the strategies and the deceits of the devil. For we are not wrestling with flesh and blood [contending only with physical opponents], but against the despotisms, against the powers, against [the master spirits who are] the world rulers of this present darkness, against the spirit forces of wickedness in the heavenly (supernatural) sphere. Therefore put on God's complete armour, that you may be able to resist and stand your ground on the evil day [of danger], and, having done all [the crisis demands], to stand [firmly in your place]. Stand therefore [hold your ground], having tightened the belt of truth around your loins and having put on the breastplate of integrity and of moral rectitude and right standing with God, and having shod your feet in preparation [to face the enemy with the firm-footed stability, the promptness, and the readiness produced by the good news] of the Gospel of peace. Lift up over all the [covering] shield of saving faith, upon which you can quench all the flaming missiles of the wicked [one]. And take the helmet of salvation and the sword that the Spirit wields, which is the Word of God" (AMP).

Through His energizing power, I have both the desire and the power to do what is pleasing in His sight. (Philippians 2:13)

"For God is working in you, giving you the desire to obey him and the power to do what pleases him" (NLT).

I have no spirit of fear and timidity, but of power, of love, and of a sound mind. (2 Timothy 1:7)

"For God did not give us a spirit of timidity (of cowardice, of craven and cringing and fawning fear), but [He has given us a spirit] of power and of love and of calm and well-balanced mind and discipline and self-control" (AMP).

I hold fast to the profession of my faith in His promises, for He is faithful to His Word. (Hebrews 10:23)

"Let us hold fast the profession of our faith without wavering; (for he is faithful that promised)."

I will never give up on God and His Word, for my reward is coming. (Hebrews 10:35)

"Do not throw away this confident trust in the Lord, no matter what happens. Remember the great reward it brings you!" (NLT).

God never changes, and He stands by His Word. (Hebrews 13:8)

"Jesus Christ is the same yesterday, today, and forever" (NLT).

My prayer of faith will heal the sick. (James 5:14–15)

"Is any sick among you? Let him call for the elders of the church; and let them pray over him, anointing him with oil in the name of the Lord: And the prayer of faith shall save the sick, and the Lord shall raise him up; and if he have committed sins, they shall be forgiven him."

I am healed by His wounds. (1 Peter 2:24)

"He personally carried away our sins in his own body on the cross so we can be dead to sin and live for what is right. You have been healed by his wounds!" (NLT).

I will have whatever I pray for, because I diligently obey His Word. (1 John 3:21–22)
"And, beloved, if our consciences (our hearts) do not accuse us [if they do not make us feel guilty and condemn us], we have confidence (complete assurance and boldness) before God, and we receive from Him whatever we ask, because we [watchfully] obey His orders [observe His suggestions and injunctions, follow His plan for us] and [habitually] practice what is pleasing to Him" (AMP).

Whatever I ask God for in accordance to His Word, I surely receive. (1 John 5:14–15)
"And we can be confident that he will listen to us whenever we ask him for anything in line with his will. And if we know he is listening when we make our requests, we can be sure that he will give us what we ask for" (NLT).

My body is healthy as my soul prospers. (3 John 1:2)
"Beloved, I wish above all things that thou mayest prosper and be in health, even as thy soul prospereth."

I'm victorious by the blood and the Word of Jesus Christ, my Lord and Saviour. (Revelation 12:11)
"And they have overcome (conquered) him by means of the blood of the Lamb and by the utterance of their testimony, for they did not love and cling to life even when faced with death [holding their lives cheap till they had to die for their witnessing]" (AMP).

SLOBODAN'S SALVATION STORY

Slobodan Krstevski was born in 1957 in Yugoslavia. From early on, he lived in the town of Kacarevo, twenty-eight kilometres north of Belgrade. His parents fought with each other frequently, both physically and verbally. As a result, he would be between them, crying and frightened. Often he would stay with family and friends for weeks and sometimes even months at a time.

When he was twelve years old, his parents divorced. Slobodan's father found another woman in Skopje, Macedonia, and Slobodan stayed with her for about six months. Later on, he was sent to stay with his grandparents in Skopje for another year and a half. At age fourteen, he was called back to stay in Kacarevo with his father, who had remarried. Then after one year, he asked his mother if he could live with her in Vienna, Austria.

During the first fifteen years of Slobodan's life, he had never heard the name of Jesus Christ. A few weeks after he arrived in Vienna, he went out walking on a rainy morning. He noticed a man distributing literature, two other men singing, and another man playing a guitar. He thought to himself, *Who are these foolish people outside in the rain?*

They were standing right in front of the store that he needed to enter. So as Slobodan walked by them, the man distributing the literature gave him some tracts. One tract had Bible verses printed in it, so he read it as he walked home. On the back of the second tract was the address of a man in Italy who offered correspondence courses on the Gospel of John, so Slobodan sent for the course materials.

The Gospel of John and the literature that he read had quite an impact on him. One of the booklets said, "If you want Jesus Christ to change your life, if you want Him to start a new thing in your heart, then pray this prayer. God will hear you, and He will change your life."

God said, *"You will seek me and find me"* (Jeremiah 29:13, NIV). And He was truthful to His Word. Slobodan prayed the sinner's prayer, and God saw the sincerity of his seeking heart. In the process of completing his correspondence course in 1972, Slobodan trusted the Lord Jesus Christ as his personal Lord and Saviour. Immediately, he wanted to practice his faith and tell others about Jesus. To him, this was a new beginning, and Slobodan has never been the same ever since.

LJILJANA'S SALVATION STORY

Before Ljiljana Krstevski was ever born, her parents were already show-ing signs of dysfunction in their relationship. They both wanted a baby very much. Her father, who was infertile, would beat her mother, think-ing it was her fault that they couldn't have children. Out of desperation, Ljiljana's mother had an affair with a neighbour, got pregnant, and in 1965, Ljiljana was born. But cultural tradition demanded that the first child be a male, so when Ljiljana's father heard that she was a girl, he wanted nothing to do with her.

Soon after, her father became a drunkard. On many occasions, he came home late at night and beat her mother. Ljiljana would be crouched in the corner of their small kitchen crying hysterically. Some-times Ljiljana and her mother would run to their neighbour's house to seek refuge. This continued until she was nine years old, at which time her parents divorced.

Her mother moved to Vienna, Austria, and Ljiljana went to live with her grandparents in Dubovac, Yugoslavia. At the age of thirteen, she started searching for parental love, so she went to live with her mother in Vienna. But when she arrived there, she learned that her mother was not the same woman that she remembered. She, too, had become a drunkard.

Ljiljana tried to earn her mother's love by achieving good marks in school. But when she gave her report card to her mother, her mother threw it on the floor and said, "I don't care." Those hurtful words devastated Ljiljana so much that she began thinking, *If no one cares, then what's the point in living?* To her, the only way out of her miserable life was to take a knife and kill herself.

Later that week, as Ljiljana was walking down a street in Vienna, she heard someone say the word "God." Then she saw a group of young people singing songs, a girl sharing her testimony, and a man preaching. That day, in 1981, she heard two things for the first time in her entire life. She learned that she was a sinner and that Jesus Christ had died for her.

Immediately, she wanted to get to know this Jesus who loved her so much. Soon after, she said the sinner's prayer with two other young people. When she finished praying, she started to cry. From that moment on, Ljiljana was completely changed. She saw that God had a purpose for her—He wanted her to live to tell her story.

PEACE WITH GOD

God's divine purpose for your life is peace and eternal life.
The Bible says, *"We have peace with God through our Lord Jesus Christ"* (Romans 5:1). Only God can provide eternal life.

You cannot have eternal life if you are separated from God.
The Bible says, *"For all have sinned; all fall short of God's glorious standard"* (Romans 3:23, NLT). God created us with a free will. But our decision to disobey God separates us from Him.

The solution to your separation from God is Jesus Christ.
The Bible says, *"For there is one God and one mediator between God and men, the man Christ Jesus"* (1 Timothy 2:5, NIV). God's only Son, Jesus Christ, died on the cross, was raised from the dead, and lives again to provide you with eternal life.

You must accept Jesus Christ as Lord and Saviour.
The Bible says, *"Behold, I stand at the door and knock. If anyone hears My voice and opens the door, I will come in to him and dine with him, and he with Me"* (Revelation 3:20, NKJV). You need to read the Word of God and learn about Jesus Christ. Then invite Him into your heart.

How do you find peace?

1) Admit that you need salvation.

2) Turn away from your sins.

3) Believe that Jesus Christ died for you and rose from the dead.

4) Pray and ask Jesus to come into your life.

May we suggest you pray?

Dear God, I know and understand from your Word that I am a sinner. I need Your forgiveness. I believe Jesus Christ died for my sins on the cross at Calvary. I want to repent and give up my sin and ask You to forgive me for the sins of my past. I invite You right now, by an act of my will, to come into my heart and transform my life. I will trust You, follow You, and acknowledge You now as my Lord and Saviour. I pray this prayer in Jesus' name. Amen.

ABOUT SHINING LIGHT MINISTRIES

Shining Light Ministries was founded by Revs. Slobodan and Ljiljana Krstevski in 1991 and is registered as a charity both in Canada (1994) and in the United States (2001). Shining Light Ministries' overall goal is to glorify God by spreading the Gospel throughout the world and making disciples of Jesus Christ. To reach our goal:

1) We produce missions-focused television programs with the Gospel message to teach God's truth on various aspects of victorious living, including: faith based on the Word of God, godly character and leadership, marriage and family issues, divine healing, goals and hard work, success and prosperity, knowing God, and growing in our new life in Him.

2) We are actively involved in evangelism, discipleship, leadership training, and theological and marriage seminars. We engage in relief work with refugees, widows, and orphaned children by providing them with much needed humanitarian aid.

3) We regularly preach to churches, businesses, women's groups, and other groups of interested people. In addition to producing CDs and

DVDs, we also publish missions news reports, books, and daily devotional messages on our website (www.SLM-Balkans.org).

Our three main areas of focus are as follows:

1) *Help the Children* allows us to distribute packages with school and hygiene items, a toy, and Christian literature to thousands of orphaned and refugee children.

2) *Feed the Christians* is a project to help our fellow brothers and sisters in Christ with food boxes and hygiene items.

3) *Reach the Refugees* gives us the opportunity to distribute food boxes to hundreds of needy refugee families and provide Christian literature that will point them to Christ.

To make an immediate donation for one or more of the above projects by Visa, MasterCard, or American Express, please call our toll-free donations number, 1-866-300-9995. Or make a secure online donation at www.SLM-Balkans.org.

Here's what others have said about Slobodan...

"Slobodan Krstevski is truly a man of vision, maturity and practical ability... The leadership here at Crossroads has found Slobodan to be a man of sterling character, careful with finances, and determined to do everything in the right way... he is meeting human need with food, medical supplies, clothing, those things that are desperately needed right now by people in the Balkans. I have a lot of confidence in Slobodan. He's a man of great integrity whom I trust implicitly. I would like to encourage you to get behind

Slobodan because he's a man of compassion, a man of love, a man of action."

—REV. DAVID MAINSE
Founder of 100 Huntley Street and Crossroads Christian Communications, Inc.

"It's our privilege to encourage you to support the work of Slobodan and Ljiljana Krstevski and Shining Light Ministries. We've known Slobodan and Ljiljana for many, many years and we've seen firsthand the work of God in their individual lives, as well as in their extended ministry. We just want to let you know that you can support them with a clear conscience knowing that they are working truly for the message of Jesus Christ to get out to their home country."

—REVS. RON AND ANN MAINSE
Hosts of 100 Huntley Street

"I've known Rev. Slobodan Krstevski and his wife, Ljiljana, for many years. I don't know a man more dedicated and absolutely concentrated and focussed on what he does and what he's doing for the people in the Balkans. When you support this man, you're supporting a man of God who's chosen and focussed on what he does. Knowing Slobodan, he won't quit. He'll keep on doing what God calls him to do in the Balkans. And what he's doing is worthwhile. I urge you with all my heart, stand behind his ministry."

—REV. DR. CAL R. BOMBAY
Cal Bombay Ministries and former
Vice-President of Missions at 100 Huntley Street

"Slobodan and Ljiljana and Shining Light Ministries have been a blessing for our church and we are thankful for the privilege and the opportunity to be part of Shining Light Ministries and to put our seed into the work of the Lord in the field of the Balkans. I want to also express appreciation to Slobodan and Ljiljana for their teaching, especially family-related, and children-related teaching, which has been a blessing for many families."

—PASTOR YAROSLAV GRINCHISHIN
Senior Pastor of Slavonic Christian Church, Buffalo, NY

"God has placed a burden on my heart for these helpless people. He has directed me to work with Shining Light Ministries to do whatever I can. I pray that God will speak to your heart so that you will help us in helping those people in whatever way you can."

—ITALO LABIGNAN
President of Canadian Sportfishing

"Slobodan, more than having just a great knowledge of the language and culture of the Balkans, goes over there with the love of Jesus. He's an ambassador to people who are in great need. He's been a bridge between Canada and that side of the world. He's totally committed to this. He has a heart for God, a love for people. And I would really encourage you to get behind his ministry."

—PASTOR CRAIG PITTS
Former Eurasia Missions Co-ordinator for the PAOC

ABOUT SHINING LIGHT MINISTRIES

"Slobodan and Ljiljana approach the ministry of Shining Light Ministries with the utmost integrity, compassion, mercy, diligence, and tremendous planning and good use of the resources that God has given to them. Because of Shining Light Ministries, the light is shining brighter and warmer in so many hundreds of thousands of lives in the Balkans and around the world."

—PASTOR SCOTT DOGGART
Regional Director-SC of WOD, PAOC

Shining Light Ministries Missions TV

Our missions TV broadcasts are packed with exciting teachings based on the Word of God for everyday life, whether it is in regards to marriage and family, parenting issues, finances, divine health, or spirituality. We also feature missions stories about the life-changing difference that God is making in the lives of thousands of needy people in the Balkans through Shining Light Ministries. Tune in to our missions TV broadcast, because God has a wonderful blessing in store for you!

Airtime Schedule (for the most current schedule check our website):

CTS: *Ontario*	Thursdays at 8:30 a.m. (EST)
	Fridays at 6:00 a.m. (EST)
	Sundays at 12:00 p.m. (EST)
CTS: *Alberta*	Tuesdays at 8:30 a.m. (MST)
	Fridays at 1:00 p.m. (MST)
	Sundays at 8:00 a.m. (MST)

GOD'S HEALING SECRETS

VisionTV	Tuesdays at 8:30 a.m. (EST)
The Miracle Channel	DAILY: Monday–Friday at 8:30 p.m. (EST) You can also watch SLM missions broadcasts online through The Miracle Channel website (www.miraclechannel.ca) at the same time.

For most updated times, check our website at: www.SLM-Balkans.org

What Viewers Are Saying About the SLM Telecast

"Several days ago, a lady from your ministry called to pray for my mother, Violet. The lady prayed for my mom with me. I know the Lord orchestrated that call, because the lady knew just what to pray for. I'm very thankful to the Lord and to her! My mom is a Christian but was struggling with so many issues for years. I felt she had some kind of stronghold, other than old age issues, which affected her ability to enjoy life, including a poor appetite. The very next time I spoke to my mom, after the lady prayed for her, something had changed. She was already eating well and joining in on all kinds of healthy social activities which she had previously shunned. So much effort has gone into helping her for so many years and yet this one prayer changed so much overnight. Everyone has noticed how much better she is doing and how much happier she is. Thank you, Lord! A testimony to the goodness of God and an answer to prayer!"

—Diane from Surrey, BC

"You prayed for my marriage and my husband came back from Germany and wants to work things out. Thank you very much for praying for us."

—Elke from Bobcaygeon, ON

"Many mornings, I really look forward to watching your program on TV. My heart goes out to the Balkans, the widows, and their children. Back here, we have so much. If everyone could give a dollar a day, what a difference it would make for this world, which is filled with suffering and starvation. God has led me to answer to your ministry the best I can financially. There are times I pray to be able to do more, but every little bit helps. God bless the both of you!"

—Brenda from Dundas, ON

"When we started to partner with SLM, I had a stack of bills on the table one morning. Instead of paying the bills, I took the money and sent it to SLM for the children in the Balkans. About the time the cheque was being cashed, I got a letter from the bank saying I had a retroactive pay being put into my bank account. I thought the bank made a mistake. It was $6,000! The Lord was showing us that you reap what you sow!

—Brent and Mildred from Medicine Hat, AB

ABOUT SARA ROZALINA KRSTEVSKI, A.R.C.T.

If you could come up with one word that would describe music artist Sara Rozalina, you'd definitely not have her pegged. This talented lady cannot be definitively labelled or boxed in.

It all began at the age of seven, when Sara started playing the piano. In 2002, Sara competed at the Burlington Rotary Music Festival and won two medals—once for first and once for second place in her group. She was also invited to play at the Grand Festival Concert as one of the finalists for the overall most promising young performer scholarships.

A classically trained pianist, Sara obtained her associate teacher's degree (A.R.C.T.) in piano performance through the Royal Conservatory of Music in 2007.

The eldest of six children, Sara is a dedicated member of her large family. Sara has also teamed up to help support Shining Light Ministries, a charity organization that provides humanitarian aid to people in the Balkan nations (the former countries of Yugoslavia).

With the ministry's primetime TV show, which her parents host and produce, Sara often takes the stage in the studio and performs her musical talents through piano and singing. Sara especially loves to share her faith through her music.

Sara has used her talents to delight audiences across Canada, the United States, Cuba, and Europe through live performances and radio plays. Sara has been privileged to share her exceptional gift on the daily Canadian Christian television show *100 Huntley Street*.

Sara's albums are available upon request for a suggested donation of $20.00 plus shipping and handling per CD. To order, call the toll-free donations number, 1-866-300-9995, or make a secure online donation at www.SLM-Balkans.org.

Check out her website at: www.sararozalina.com.

Discography of Sara Rozalina Krstevski

Soli Deo Gloria. This beautiful collection of the masters, like Bach, Chopin, and Mozart, will inspire you to say, as the great composer J.S. Bach usually wrote at the end of each music composition, "Glory to God alone."

Above All. Let your faith in God be strengthened through powerful worship. In this collection of anointed singing and playing by Sara, listen about the wonderful love of God for you in pieces such as "Above All" and "Here I Am to Worship."

The Promise. Develop a closer, more intimate relationship with the Lord through this wonderful, inspirational collection of piano and orchestral music, such as "Joyful, Joyful, We Adore Thee" and "Standing on the Promises of God." Sara plays the piano at eleven years of age like any adult pro would.

SLM DAILY DEVOTIONALS

Shining Light Ministries offers practical and biblical teachings for every-day life as part of the ministry's daily devotionals, which can be found on the website (www.SLM-Balkans.org). Now you can be blessed every day of the year through our inspirational teachings from the Word of God.

Every day offers a different scriptural passage and a short teaching to help you be successful in your life and your walk with the Lord. Rev. Slobodan Krstevski teaches on a variety of different subjects relating to spirituality, relationships, finances, raising children, and overall well-being.

The Krstevski Family
Back Row: Joshua, Peter, David, and Slobodan.
Front Row: Ljiljana, Deborah, Elisabeth, and Sara.

GOD'S HEALING SECRETS

God sends His Word and heals us! Your body is the temple of the Holy Spirit. Sickness does not belong to you. It's time to stop calling it "my sickness" and say goodbye to it once and for all.

A lot of people, both young and old, expect to be sick and unhealthy as they get older. But Dr. Slobodan Krstevski wants to encourage you not to accept any sickness as a "final say" in your life but to declare in agreement with the Word of God that you are free from sickness and that you are blessed with divine health in Jesus' name!

Dr. Krstevski provides balanced answers to issues of divine and natural healing. By examining the healing ministry in the Old Testament, of Jesus, and of the Early Church, Dr. Krstevski provides a biblical basis for his belief in divine healing.

This book's purpose is to provide you with knowledge and insight to help you understand how you can receive healing from a supernatural and natural perspective.

Dr. Krstevski also shares from his own personal insights and experiences, which will inspire and encourage you to take hold of God's health plan for you!

God's Healing Secrets is available upon request for a suggested donation to Shining Light Ministries in the amount of $39.95 plus shipping and handling. To order, call the toll-free donations number, 1-866-300-9995. You can also order the book or make a secure online donation at www.SLM-Balkans.org.

"Slobodan, I found your book, *God's Healing Secrets*, to be a wonderful guide for everybody who needs health, both in the physical and spiritual sense."

—DR. BENITO MUÑOZ, MD
Tijuana, Mexico

"I have personally applied some of the biblical truths on healing spoken about in Dr. Slobodan Krstevski's book and I was healed."

—DR. IRENA VITANOVSKA, MD
Skopje, Macedonia

BLESS YOUR CHILDREN TO SUCCEED

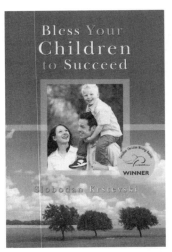

This inspirational resource is a must-have for all current and expecting parents. As Rev. Slobodan Krstevski shares several key elements of successful parenting, you can learn how to equip your children with everything they need to become successful. This book won an award from The Word Guild as the best book on the subject in Canada in its category.

In this condensed but informative text, Rev. Krstevski discusses several key elements that parents can utilize in their own parenting to equip their children with everything they need to become successful.

Readers are given a peek inside the life of a family who has learned to apply the Word of God in every aspect of their lives. As Rev. Krstevski shares some of his own personal stories, parents can identify with his experiences and will be inspired to employ his principles in their own parenting techniques.

This book is a great tool for all parents who desire to provide their children with Biblical values to fulfill all that their potential holds. It's full of godly wisdom, inspiring stories, and practical guidance to help people enjoy their journey as parents.

Bless Your Children to Succeed is available upon request for a suggested donation to Shining Light Ministries in the amount of $20.00 plus shipping and handling. To order, call the toll-free donations number, 1-866-300-9995. You can also order the book or make a secure online donation at www.SLM-Balkans.org.

"I encourage you to glean from Slobodan's tried-and-proven insights for establishing a healthy, God-centred family life."

—REV. RON MAINSE
Host of 100 Huntley Street

"Slobodan and Ljiljana have some of the most well-adjusted, happy, and productive kids I've ever met in my life. I guess what they're doing is working. You can't do better than that!"

—JIM FISHER
Businessman, Burlington, ON

FROM THE CURSE OF DEBT TO FINANCIAL FREEDOM: SEVEN PRINCIPLES OF PROSPERITY

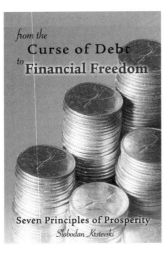

from the **Curse of Debt** *to* **Financial Freedom**

Seven Principles of Prosperity

Slobodan Krstevski

Get ready to break the curse of debt over your life and step into the financial freedom you've always wanted! Rather than just working for your money, you can make your money work for you. In this powerful and dynamic book, Rev. Slobodan Krstevski reveals how you can turn your stressful money troubles into an overflow of prosperity! God doesn't want you to live in the land of "not enough" but in the land of "more than enough"—the land of abundance.

If you decide today that you want to change your financial situation, God will give you all the wisdom you need to do so. He will give you the power to create wealth. But creating it does not depend on your circumstances, other people, or your life history. It depends on you and God. When you and God join forces, nothing is going to stop you from prospering, because through Christ, you can do all things. This powerful book will teach you how to break the curse of debt over your life and step into financial freedom!

From the Curse of Debt to Financial Freedom: Seven Principles of Prosperity is available upon request for a suggested donation to Shining Light Ministries in the amount of $25.00 plus shipping and handling. To order, call the toll-free donations number, 1-866-300-9995. You can also order the book or make a secure online donation at www.SLM-Balkans.org.

"You've captured the essence of the financial conundrum that plagues humanity, and you present clear, pragmatic solutions to the burdens that many feel today."

—ARMANDO DAVID VACCA

Dipl.B., C.F.P., R.F.P., Certified Financial Planner, Registered Financial Planner, Founder/Owner of A.D. Vacca & Associates Financial Planning Group

"The insights of this book give it a strong edge over many others of its kind."

—J. DOUG HAWKINS, FICB, MBA

HIS OR HER CUP OF LOVE: SEVEN STEPS TO A GREAT MARRIAGE

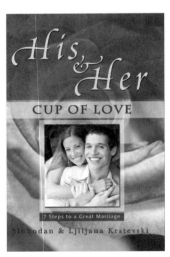

Reflecting on their own experiences and the wisdom found in the Word of God, Revs. Slobodan and Ljiljana Krstevski discuss the differences between husbands and wives and the steps needed to ensure a great marriage. Whether you're preparing for marriage or you've been married for years, this award-winning book is an excellent tool to have in your home.

Being happily married to a loving and devoted spouse can really be paradise on this side of heaven. The romantic love songs we've heard, the movies that show the magic of falling in love, and the fairy-tale love stories we've been told as children all portray that blissful experience of being in love.

HIS OR HER CUP OF LOVE

The Scriptures speak very highly of love as well, so much so that a relationship between Christ and the Church is compared with the relationship between a husband and wife and is used to convey the message of love (Ephesians 5:22–33). Romantic love is not only important in the world; it's also important to God. And if it's important to God, we should give it a significant role in our lives, too. We should do whatever we can to increase our knowledge and understanding of romantic love if we are to indeed experience the blissfulness found in the paradise this side of heaven called marriage.

His and Her Cup of Love: Seven Steps to a Great Marriage is a tool to enable you to learn everything it takes to make a marriage successful. I'm positive that if you prayerfully read, meditate upon, and apply the biblically-based teachings discussed in this book, you will indeed have a great marriage.

His and Her Cup of Love: Seven Steps to a Great Marriage is available upon request for a suggested donation to Shining Light Ministries in the amount of $39.95 plus shipping and handling. To order, call the toll-free donations number, 1-866-300-9995. You can also order the book or make a secure online donation at www.SLM-Balkans.org.

"Here is a must-read book for those thinking of marriage or are married. Slobodan and Ljiljana have put together a comprehensive, biblical-based examination of what it takes to make a marriage great. Through research and personal understanding, this book provides an outstanding opportunity for couple t o learn how to be married successfully."

—MARK LAING

Counsellor & Certified, Pastoral Counsellor Bayridge Family Center, Burlington, ON
Former host of "Family Matters"

"I would recommend this book to any teenager, adult, or anybody who would be interested in educating themselves on marriage… would be happy to give this book to family, friends, and clients."

—PHYTOS DEMETRI

Head Trainer, Alliance Fitness Corporation

171

AUDIO TEACHING CDS

Become inspired, motivated, and empowered to develop a stronger, more faith-filled relationship with God by feeding your spirit with the wonderful messages that God has led Rev. Slobodan Krstevski to share with you. These audio teaching CDs are packed with Word-based principles to help you learn various aspects of victorious Christian living regarding spirituality, marriage and family, finances, physical health, and more. Release the power of the Holy Spirit into every area of your life by equipping yourself with biblical knowledge for successful living.

As you listen to Rev. Krstevski preach the uncompromised Word of God, these messages will not only motivate you to become everything God intended for you to be but will empower you to possess everything God intended you to have. It's time to take what's rightfully yours as a joint heir with Christ Jesus. Healing, prosperity, freedom, power, and victory all belong to you. Find out how you can take possession of the very things God is waiting for you to take.

These powerful Bible-based messages will provide you with what you need to overcome any obstacle you may face. So bring the Word of God and the power of the Holy Spirit into your home, your car, or your office by ordering Rev. Krstevski's audio teaching CDs today!

Available Audio Teaching CDs

Confessing the Word

Faith Cometh by Hearing

Abide in Me and My Word

The Power to Create Wealth

The Keys to Successful Marriage

For more CD Teachings visit our website.

These audio teaching CDs are available upon request for a suggested donation of $10.00 plus shipping and handling per CD. When you order, please clearly identify which CD(s) you would like. To order our other resources, call the toll-free donations number, 1-866-300-9995. You can also order our books, music CDs, or make a secure online donation at www.SLM-Balkans.org.

Feedback Form

If this book has impacted you in any way or if you (or someone you know) has received Christ and prayed the prayer of salvation after reading this book, please let us know. We would love to hear from you. Also, if there is a topic you would like to see published in a future edition, please write your suggestions and comments in the space provided. Make a photocopy and then send this feedback form to Shining Light Ministries:

In Canada:
P.O. Box 93035
Burlington, ON
L7M 4A3

In U.S.A.:
P.O. Box 1133
Grand Island, NY
14072

Comments:

_____
_____
_____
_____
_____
_____
_____

• Yes, I have received Jesus Christ as my personal Lord and Saviour after reading this book, and I have prayed the sinner's prayer.

Name: _____

Address: _____

City: _____ Prov/State: _____

PC/Zip: _____ Tel: (_____)_____

Order Form (Page 1)

Please complete and return this entire order form to Shining Light Ministries at the addresses on the feedback form.

	Items		Price	Quantity	Total
Music CDs	The Promise		$20.00		
	Above All		$20.00		
	Soli Deo Gloria		$20.00		
Books	God's Healing Secrets		$39.95		
	Bless Your Children to Succeed		$20.00		
	From the Curse of Debt to Financial Freedom		$25.00		
	His and Her Cup of Love		$39.95		
Audio Teaching CDs	Confessing the Word		$10.00		
	Abide in Me and My Word		$10.00		
	The Power to Create Wealth		$10.00		
	Faith Cometh by Hearing		$10.00		
	The Keys to Successful Marriage		$10.00		
Subtotal					
Shipping and Handling		**CAN**	**U.S.A.**		
$10.00 and under		$4.95	$6.95		
$10.01-$25.00		$9.00	$12.00		
$25.01-50.00		$12.00	$16.00		
$50.01-$75.00		$14.00	$18.00		
$75.01-$100.00		$16.00	$20.00		
$100.01 and more, add for each additional $50 purchase		$12.00	$14.00		
Total					

• I would also like to give a special offering to support the outreaches of Shining Light Ministries. My offering in the amount of _____ is included in the **Total Amount to be Charged** on the following page.

Please turn over and complete Page 2 of this order form.

Order Form (Page 2)

After you have completed Page 1 of the Order Form indicating all the products you would like to receive, please fill out Page 2 to indicate your method of payment and personal information.

Total Amount to be Charged is: $_____
(This amount is the Subtotal for all products ordered including S&H and, if applicable, your special offering to Shining Light Ministries.)

I'm paying by:

• Visa   • MasterCard   • Amex

Card Number: _____

Expiry date: _____ / _____   Today's Date: _____

Name (as printed on the card): _____

Signature: _____

Personal Information

Name: _____

Address: _____

City: _____   Prov/State: _____

PC/Zip: _____   Tel: (_____)_____

E-mail: _____

If you are making your payment by cheque, please make all cheques payable to Shining Light Ministries.

Please note: *We can only issue a tax receipt for your missions offering at tax time. We cannot issue a tax receipt for the products ordered due to Canada Revenue Agency's "Fair Market Value" (FMV) policy. Thank you for your understanding in this matter.*

Dear Friend,

Wherever we go, we meet people who are struggling with life's challenges. People have problems with children, marriage, finances, and health. They face many uncertainties. Everywhere we go, we find people who are looking for answers. You and I have the key to those answers—it is found in the Word of God and His love for them.

What we need to do is give that key to them. Our way to encourage others and to share the Word of God and His love for them is to share these books: *God's Healing Secrets, His and Her Cup of Love: Seven Steps to a Great Marriage, Bless Your Children to Succeed*, and *From the Curse of Debt to Financial Freedom: Seven Principles of Prosperity*. Not only can they find a prayer of salvation if they don't already know the Lord, but they can be mightily equipped to deal with the important issues of life. The stories we share are about what God has done in and through our own lives. These stories can lead others to live victorious lives as they, too, experience the goodness and faithfulness of God.

So why not pass this book along to a friend, neighbour, family member, or even a stranger? After you've read this book, pray that the Lord will lead you to whom He wants you to share this book with. Pray that the testimonies and the Word will become alive in their hearts. Stand in faith that the person you've shared this book with will understand that God has answers for him or her.

It would be exciting to hear your reports as to what happened once you passed this book along. By reading this book, did someone pray the prayer of salvation, experience the love of God, or gain wisdom to resolve a marriage, family, financial, or health issue? Please let us know!

Ljiljana and I are joining our faith with yours as you step out and pass along this book as an expression of God's love to the people around you.

Remember, God loves you.

Rev. Dr. Slobodan Krstevski

ENDNOTES

[1] Bruce J. Klein, *This Wonderful Lengthening Lifespan*, Immortality Institute,

http://www.imminst.org/forum/index.php?act=ST&f=67&t=680&s (January 7, 2003) as quoted in V. Kannisto, *Development of Oldest-Old Mortality, 1950-1990* (Denmark: Odense University Press, 1994) online at http://www.demogr.mpg.de/Papers/Books/Mono...1/OldestOld.htm.

[2] http://www.topnews.in/health/bitterness-and-resentment-can-make-you-sick-german-experts-warn-22605

[3] Ibid.

[4] If we have advanced so far into sickness from the divine health plan, the course of action should be to use medical science, both its advice and corresponding treatment. I would, however, first look into natural, alternative ways that might be able to help. But I would at the same time proceed with the standard medical treatment after I've fully availed myself of all the necessary information regarding the benefits and negative effects of the said treatment. You need divine guidance to know exactly what course of action to take in any given situation. However, be aware that medical science has its limitations and can often lead to

misdiagnosis. Medical science can't *cure* you. Your immune system does that.

5 The prayer shawl, called the *tallit* (also pronounced *tallis*), is the most authentic Jewish garment. It was made out of linen or wool and cut in a rectangular shape. It also had special fringes called *Tzitzit* (tassels) on each of the four corners. Actually, the purpose of the garment was to hold the *Tzitzit*. According to Numbers 15:37–41, the Lord spoke to Moses to instruct the Israelites to make themselves fringes on the corners of their garments in order to recall the commandments of the Lord and to observe them. So the purpose of the *tallit* was to hold the *Tzitzit*. The purpose of the *Tzitzit* (according to the *Torah*) was to remind us of God's commandments. So when the woman who had a blood flow for twelve years touched the tassels (*Tzitzit*) of the prayer shawl (*Tallit*), she was actually figuratively touching the Word of God.

6 Pat Farrell Ph.D., "The Power of Human Touch," WebMDBlog, http://blogs.webmd.com/anxiety-and-stress-management/2006/02/power-of-human-touch.html (February 1, 2006).

7 Quotationspage.com and Michael Moncur, *Quotations by Author Hippocrates (460 BC–377 BC)*, http://www.quotationspage.com/quotes/hippocrates (1994–2007).

8 Curtis Rush, "Obesity Shortens Kids' Life Spans: Report," *Toronto Star*, March 27, 2007, (http://www.thestar.com/News/article/196461). A new report entitled "Healthy Weight for Healthy Kids" suggests that the childhood obesity "epidemic" is so disturbing that today's children will become the first generation in some time to have a shorter life expectancy than their parents. Weight problems can lead to Type 2 diabetes, heart attack, stroke, joint problems, and mental health issues. According to recent data, twenty-six percent of Canadians aged 2–17 are overweight or obese. An even more disturbing figure is the fact that only nine percent of parents recognize their children to be obese or overweight.

[9] Suzanne MacNevin, "Anorexia vs. Obesity in North America," lilithgallery.com,

http://www.lilithgallery.com/articles/2005/anorexia_vs_obesity.html.
[10] Ibid.
[11] Hayley Mick, "Do You Know Who Your Doctor's 'Friends' Are?" *Globe and Mail*, April 24, 2007,

(http://www.theglobeandmail.com/servlet/story/RTGAM.20070424.wxlpharma24/BNStory/specialScienceandHealth). According to a paper entitled "Following the Script: How Drug Reps Make Friends and Influence Doctors," co-authored by an ex-U.S. drug representative and a physician, pharmaceutical salespeople use carefully honed psychological techniques on doctors in their efforts to sell more pills. As a result, they may be influencing the way doctors choose to prescribe drugs. The paper reveals that the strategies of some pharmaceutical reps include scouring the doctor's office for novels, sports equipment, and even religious symbols in order to use those cues to "establish a personal connection." Experts say that consumers are at risk because physicians may be influenced to prescribe medication too often and they may choose newer, more expensive drugs over older drugs with track records.
[12] WrongDiagnosis.com, "How Common Are Medical Mistakes?" http://www.wrongdiagnosis.com/mistakes/common.htm
[13] Quotationspage.com and Michael Moncur, *Quotations by Author Hippocrates (460 BC–377 BC)*,

http://www.quotationspage.com/quotes/hippocrates (1994–2007).
[14] R. Morgan Griffin, "Give Your Body a Boost—With Laughter: Why, For Some, Laughter is the Best Medicine," WebMD,

http://women.webmd.com/guide/give-your-body-boost-with-laughter (April 10, 2006).
[15] Tammy Darling, "Water Works," *Vibrant Life*, January 2001 (http://findarticles.com/p/articles/mi_m0826/is_1_17/ai_69371786).
[16] Dr. Don Colbert, MD, *The Seven Pillars of Health* (Lake Mary, Florida: Siloam, A Strang Company, 2007), pp. 5–35.

[17] Ibid.

[18] Natural Resources Defence Council, "Bottled Water: Pure Drink or Pure Hype?" http://www.nrdc.org/water/drinking/nbw.asp (March 1999).

[19] Quotationspage.com and Michael Moncur, *Quotations by Author Hippocrates (460 BC-377 BC),*

http://www.quotationspage.com/quotes/hippocrates (1994-2007).

[20] Morphine is produced from opium, which is derived from poppy plants. Most medicines used today, however, are manufactured through chemical processes (cf.

http://www.medicalnewstoday.com/articles/9997.php).

[21] Dr. Kurt W. Donsbach, "Cancer Restraint Diet," Santa Monica Health Institute (Revised edition 2004), p. 5.

[22] National Sleep Foundation, "What Happens When You Sleep?" http://www.sleepfoundation.org/site/c.huIXKjM0IxF/b.2419159/k.A8 17/What_Happens_When_You_Sleep.htm (accessed April 30, 2007).

[23] National Sleep Foundation, "Myths and Facts about Sleep," http://www.sleepfoundation.org/site/c.huIXKjM0IxF/b.2419251/k.27 73/Myths__and_Facts__About_Sleep.htm (accessed April 30, 2007).

[24] Ibid.

[25] National Sleep Foundation, "What Happens When You Sleep?" http://www.sleepfoundation.org/site/c.huIXKjM0IxF/b.2419159/k.A8 17/What_Happens_When_You_Sleep.htm (accessed April 30, 2007).

[26] Quotationspage.com and Michael Moncur, *Quotations by Author Hippocrates (460 BC–377 BC),*

http://www.quotationspage.com/quotes/hippocrates (1994–2007).

[27] Dr. Lynn Hardy, N.D., C.N.C., *Why is Every Other American Chronically Ill?* Global College of Natural Medicine,

http://www.gcnm.com/colon_cleansing_detox.html (2003).

[28] Quotationspage.com and Michael Moncur, *Quotations by Author Hippocrates (460 BC–377 BC),*

http://www.quotationspage.com/quotes/hippocrates (1994–2007).

[29] cf. George H. Tomlinson, *Effects of Acid Deposition on the Forests of Europe-North America* (CRC Press, 1990).

[30] Suzanne MacNevin, "Anorexia vs. Obesity in North America," lilithgallery.com,

http://www.lilithgallery.com/articles/2005/anorexia_vs_obesity.html.

[31] Roy Walford, *Beyond the 120 Year Diet* (New York, New York: Four Walls Eight Windows, 2000), pp. 45-49, referenced in K.C. Craichy, *Super Health* (Minneapolis, Minnesota: Bronze Bow Publishing, 2005), p. 57.

[32] Heidi Hardman, *Where the Brain Organizes Actions*, Cell Press, http://www.eurekalert.org/pub_releases/2006-06/cp-wtb060806.php. (June 14, 2006). The researchers, Etienne Koechlin and Thomas Jubault of Université Pierre et Marie Curie and Ecole Normale Supérieure, described their experiments in the June 15, 2006 issue of *Neuron*.